Life Was Simpler Then

Other books by Loula Grace Erdman

THE YEARS OF THE LOCUST

LONELY PASSAGE

THE EDGE OF TIME

THREE AT THE WEDDING

THE FAR JOURNEY

THE SHORT SUMMER

MANY A VOYAGE

THE MAN WHO TOLD THE TRUTH

THE WIND BLOWS FREE

THE WIDE HORIZON

THE GOOD LAND

ROOM TO GROW

Life Was Simpler Then

BY LOULA GRACE ERDMAN

Dodd, Mead & Company
New York

"*Hello, Central*" *is based on an article that appeared in* The Rural New-Yorker *and the October 1952 issue of* The Reader's Digest. "*And on the Seventh Day—*" *is based on an article,* "Religion Used to Be Such Fun," *that appeared in the February 1959 issue of* Christian Herald. "We Did It for the Town" *is based on an article that appeared in the August 1958 issue of* Christian Herald. "Feet That Went to School" *is based on an article,* "The Schools That Grew America," *that appeared in the September 1962 issue of* Christian Herald. "*Summer's Sweetness, Stored Away*" *is based on an article,* "Apple Butter Time," *that appeared in the October 17, 1948 issue of* Empire Magazine. "They Took the Children With Them" *is based on an article that appeared in the December 4, 1949 issue of* Empire Magazine.

Contents

Spring

1. Heroes in Overalls   3
2. Hello, Central   17
3. Not a Speck of Dirt   28
4. Friends of the Family   39

Summer

5. The Ice Cream Supper   59
6. And on the Seventh Day—   71
7. Thicker Than Water   87
8. We Did It for the Town   97

Fall

9. Feet That Went to School   109
10. "The House Will Come to Order—"   120
11. Summer's Sweetness, Stored Away   127
12. Reading Aloud   134

Winter

13. "The Least of These—"   147
14. They Took the Children With Them   159
15. Winter Harvest   167
16. But Once a Year   177

For Blanche and James
and
for all the rest of the kin who will, I hope,
say, "Yes, that's exactly the way it was."

Spring

I.

Heroes in Overalls

IT would be well along in February when Papa would come home from town and say, "Well, I hired a man today."

Then we knew spring had really come at last, and pretty soon things would be humming on the farm. We couldn't be entirely sure until then, even though Mama had begun to save eggs for early hatching, and seed catalogues, with their surrealistically bright pictures, had already found their way to our library table.

"Oh, Papa," we children would cry in a single breath, "a new hand! What's he like?"

"Well," Papa would hedge, "he showed up at the Store wanting a job. Looks like a good worker, so I hired him."

Which wasn't at all what we wanted to know. The Store, where Papa sold implements, automobiles, and suchlike, was close to the railroad station. Jobless men were forever swinging off freight trains and wandering over to ask for work. In our present complicated age, nobody in his right mind would hire a man without taking a look at his references, social security number, case history, and in some cases, the results of his aptitude test. But in those innocent days, if a man said he wanted work and Papa happened to need help, there was a meeting of minds on the spot.

Looking back on the situation now, I wonder that we weren't all murdered in our beds or subjected to some atrocity or other.

For Papa blithely took off to the Store almost every weekday afternoon, leaving the new hired man working at the task assigned him. I am sure it never occurred to him that Mama and we three children—or Mama alone, if school happened to be in session—could be in any danger at the hands of this stranger who, for all we knew, might have escaped from Alcatraz, eluded his keepers in a mental hospital, or just dropped in from another planet. I think we children would have welcomed any such condition, thinking it would make the newcomer different and, therefore, more interesting.

We would have believed the ex-con when he told us he had been framed; we would have thought the mental case funny-ha-ha (as distinguished from funny-peculiar); we would have been enchanted by the visitor from outer space, begging him for details about his planet-world. That was the criterion we three children used in judging a hand. He must be a teller of tales. In the light of experience gained in later years, I doubt very much that our narrators stuck to facts. Attention as flattering as ours might well spur on a storyteller to describe feats not entirely substantiated by actual events.

They were the twentieth-century troubadours, those itinerant hired men, materializing out of nowhere as it were, landing at our place like migratory birds in flight, resting briefly while they stored up strength before going on. Nobody ever thought of them as tramps, although perhaps in a sense they were just that. Surely somewhere they had families, roots, ties. But of these we rarely learned. Occasionally one stayed on in the community, perhaps even marrying and settling down on a place of his own. But for the most part they came to us briefly, told us wonderful stories about the Great World, and then went on their way. We had no TV then, no radio, and only an occasional movie. We didn't feel any lack, for we had our Richard Haliburton right there, giving us travelogues, and all for free.

For instance, there was Toby.

He came home with Papa one evening just as Mama was putting supper on the table. A small man, with deeply tanned skin, he had an ageless look about him. He might have been twenty, or he could have been forty. His eyes had the look of one who is forever peering into distant skylines.

"This is Toby," Papa announced. (Now that I think about it, we rarely knew, or cared about, a hired man's surname.)

"Missis," Toby said (never did he call Mama anything else), "Missis, I can tell I am going to like this place fine. Reminds me of a café I used to eat at in Paris. May I ask a favor, though? I have to have my Java, three times a day. Coffee, that is," he finished.

I flew for the coffeepot, flashing a quick look at Sister. This one was a talker—he'd do.

From our point of view, he was all right. Papa pronounced him a good worker. Only Mama complained.

"He talks all the time," she said. "And that eternal coffee. I buy three times as much as I ordinarily need."

Coffee, indeed! A small price to pay for the delight of listening to Toby. Even now I can remember his stories of the strange places he had seen. The heat of a Missouri summer's evening would be closing down like a tent as we children lay on pallets, looking up at the moon-washed or star-studded sky. Papa chose to lie full length on the grass, maintaining it was good for most of the ills to which flesh was heir. Mama sat in a chair. Toby reclined, arms linked around his knees, not looking at any of us, his voice droning on and on, a curious monotone blending with the chirping of the crickets, the croaking of the frogs, and the occasional calling of the night birds. Mama might say his talking tired her, but we noticed she always made it a point to be where she could listen, too.

New Orleans and Salt Lake City, Paris and Cairo, London and Timbuktu came to life while we listened. We climbed the Matterhorn with him, waited for the pin to drop in the Mormon Temple. We heard the roar of Victoria Falls, called Thundering Smoke by the natives. Small black men, poisoned spears clutched in uplifted hands, crept across our peaceful middle west lawn. I noticed that Brother, for all he was five years old and brave as the next one, slipped closer to Papa. So I begged Toby to tell us about New York, where no known cannibals roamed.

He told us. Big ships steamed slowly in, while straining eyes sought the first glimpse of Liberty guarding the harbor. Subways rushed and roared, with teeming millions swarming on the streets above them. Sidewalk merchants vended their wares and millionaires came sedately out of St. Thomas' from a fashionable wedding. The Flatiron Building, with its triangular shape, was right there on our own croquet court.

"By the way," Toby said, "when I came through Kansas City, I saw a building shaped like old Flatiron. What would it be?"

"The Westgate Hotel," Papa told him, "where Main Street seems to divide."

When a few months later we went on a family outing to Kansas City, I turned a cold shoulder on Swope Park with its sunken gardens and zoo, demanding to be taken to the Westgate. Once there I stood in a kind of trance, seeing, as plain as anything, the Flatiron Building in New York City. It was at least a hundred times as big as the building before me, with structures crowded on every side of it, so tall the sun never shone through to the walks below. And on those shaded sidewalks people teemed, thicker than flies on a spot of jelly. It must be so, for Toby had told us.

When fall came, he left.

"Think I'll try Portugal this year, Missis," he confided to Mama. "I've a mind to see cork growing."

For the most part, it is impossible to remember the order in which these hired men came to us. Someway, they seem to merge in my memory, so that they are all of a piece, their coming marking no special summer in my life; I can't remember whether I was six or sixteen when this or that one came. But I do recall the order of Izzy's appearance quite well, for he succeeded Toby. Although he was a wheelhorse for work, his conversation was limited to the most rudimentary and utilitarian phrases. After Toby, he was an utter washout, so far as we children were concerned. The first night at supper he ventured his one remark for the evening. It was, even before Papa asked the blessing, "Bread!" And, linking wish with action, he stood up and speared a slice with his fork.

We did not expect Mama to reprimand him, for after all, a hired man's table manners came under the heading of his own business. In our day, we had seen some hitherto unsuspected versions of the ancient art of feeding one's face, but before us we now had some entirely new variations. Izzy ate with motions which were neither scooping nor raking nor shoveling, yet partook faintly of all three. We might have suspended all our own eating to watch him except that the man himself was more unusual than his feeding habits. Small almost to the point of dwarfishness, he was perfectly, completely, entirely bald. I mean, there wasn't even one hair, one patch of fuzz on his head. However, as if in compensation for this lack, he had the most luxurious walrus mustache I have ever seen. It was so large, one wondered how it escaped throwing him forward on his nose, an accident which would have been most lamentable, for on that nose was a wart, large and purple. Mama managed to keep Sister and me in line with a Look, but Brother, being younger or perhaps sitting out of range, began, "What is that on your—ouch!"

So we knew Mama's thumb and forefinger had put across the admonition. He didn't speak again during the meal, to Izzy at least, but every time he raised his puzzled eyes they fell straight on that imperfection of the new hired man.

Supper finished, Izzy retired to his room, the one reserved for "hands." A small wooden building, set off from the house, it was called the summer kitchen, although it was never used in that capacity, either in summer or in winter. A vestigial structure, harking back to the days when cooking was done by slaves in a room set apart from the Big House and then hurried to the family dining room via small black children standing around waiting for that very purpose. I did not realize how much of an American heritage that summer kitchen was until I went to Mount Vernon and saw the one there.

From Izzy's room came, presently, great sounds of pounding

and hammering, almost as if the cooks of a bygone age had come back to life, taking up their pounding of beaten biscuits, their beating of steaks. We all wondered, Mama a bit uneasily, what was going on. The next morning, after Izzy had gone to the field, we went out to make his bed and tidy the room and, naturally, to make investigations. There was nothing amiss—he had even made his own bed, neat as a woman.

"Maybe," Sister ventured, "he was taking exercises."

The noises continued for the better part of a week. At the end of that time, Izzy emerged bearing two pairs of boots—one a variety known as "gum boots," the other a type called "felts." From each he had cut the tops and then neatly replaced them on the other pair. Now he held up the results of his labors, pride in his accomplishment loosening his tongue so that he got out the longest sentence he uttered during his stay with us.

"I make the boots, all right," he bragged. And then, overcome either by his eloquence or his cobbling, he repeated his statement, "I make the boots, see."

Papa retired in haste to the tool shed and left Mama to congratulate the artisan.

I think Izzy liked us well enough and might have stayed on until fall had not an unfortunate incident occurred. A small cousin came to spend the night. Nobody had the presence of mind to warn her ahead of time about Izzy's appearance or table manners, so she was quite unprepared for what she saw. All during supper she regarded him with bright, unwinking eyes. Even in our nervous apprehension we could understand her amazement. She was sitting out of Mama's reach, but I doubt that a Look or even a pinch would have got through to her.

"What's your name?" she finally asked.

We were surprised that Izzy answered her, but he did.

Mama tried in vain to shift the conversation. The child refused to be diverted.

"Well, Izzy," she said firmly. "I must say you are a messy kid at the table."

Sister and I collided as we left the room. We threw ourselves on the sofa in the living room and crammed pillows into our mouths to stifle our mirth. On no account was Izzy to be offended, with the corn in the stage where it needed immediate attention.

But the damage was done. Brother, either thinking the need for caution was over or, what was more likely, unable to restrain himself, now broke in.

"A messy kid," he chortled. "Ha-ha-ha—"

He was off, the young cousin joining him. Mama evidently couldn't pinch them both at the same time, or maybe she knew it was too late, or maybe she was just tired of Izzy. Or, maybe, he was tired of us. The next morning he asked for his pay and left, wearing one pair of boots, the other slung over his shoulder.

I guess Papa was desperate, being left in the middle of laying by corn, for he came home that evening from the Store with a most unlikely-looking prospect for a hand, especially at this busy time. He was too old for farm work, and besides, he was the sort who would be more at home with a book in his hand than he would be sitting on the seat of a plow. Even Sister sensed that.

"He looks like an important person," she said. "Like a general in our history book."

So, The General he became. Papa explained the nickname. "You know how children are . . ." he said, his voice trailing off.

"It's quite all right," The General said, bowing to us in a way we knew knights would bow in court. I instinctively stood straighter, as I had read that princesses were taught to do.

He spoke in a crisp, precise manner, alien and unfamiliar to our ears. It was not until long afterward that I read about Miss Mitford and her U and Non-U, but even then I knew The General was well ahead of most people.

Actually, things turned out better than we could have hoped for. The General, although older than any other hand we ever had, was still strong enough and able enough to plow the corn, which was what we needed done at the moment. And as a talker, we could have asked for nothing better. He and Papa, himself a great reader, used to have some fine discussions. I think I can trace my pleasure in good conversation back to that summer. I remember sitting entranced as the two of them discussed the theory that the North American Indian was really a descendant of one of the lost tribes of Israel.

"Some say the continents were connected ages ago," Papa said. "And, even if they weren't, the distance is short. They tell me on clear nights the lights of Asia can be seen across the Bering Strait."

I spent the next day mooning over my geography and had to be threatened with punishment if I didn't take my turn at doing dishes.

Some nights they fell to talking of the stars. The General named them for us, and we got cricks in our necks from looking up so long and steadfastly. I wanted desperately to be lost in the woods so that I could find my way home by aid of the North Star and maybe save the whole family from wolves or starvation or some other dire danger. When the talk turned to light rays and the ages it took them to reach the earth from their parent star, I was a frank unbeliever. Still, it must have put its mark on me, for today I think of the great age of space exploration not in scientific terms alone, but as something wrapt in poetry and wonder and beauty. And, looking up to trace, hopefully, the flash of a satellite across the sky, I am once more a little girl and The General is telling me the story of the stars God put there at the beginning of time. And, even as then, I am struck with the magnificence of it all, and the world's smallness (and mine) and the bigness of the universe and of God.

Mama liked The General, too. He called her Lady, and was unfailing in his courtesy and graciousness. Even so, she couldn't conceal her surprise at one of his first requests.

The first afternoon, he came to the house promptly at four.

"My goodness," Mama said, "has something happened—"

Of course, she had visions of a horse falling dead in the traces or the plow breaking—or worst of all, that The General had decided to quit, with the corn not half laid by.

"I have come for my tea, Lady," he explained, "if, of course, you are not too busy to prepare it. Neither milk nor sugar, thank you, and plain bread and butter will do nicely."

"Your tea," Mama echoed blankly. "Your tea—oh, yes, your tea. I'll fix it.'"

Except for iced tea in summer, which we consumed by the gallon, we were not tea drinkers. But Mama found the cannister and set the water boiling. Sister ran to the icebox for butter and I sliced bread, a bit thick, for I was excited. Tea! Just like I had read about in English novels.

After that, we had afternoon tea, with us children joining in the ritual. We were accustomed to a fourth meal, served in the afternoon on the occasion of hay harvest or some other more difficult work. But this was different; it had all the air of a social occasion, almost like serving refreshments to the Ladies Aid when it met at our house. Mama never complained once about the extra work; I think she liked it herself.

There was one day, however, when we didn't have tea.

On a Saturday evening, The General had gone off to town, his first month's pay in his pocket. (Only he called it "village" and for some reason I couldn't quite explain, I felt affronted. Village, indeed!) He did not get back in time for breakfast, and the meal was strangely lonesome for us. We were dressing for Sunday school, an enterprise usually attended by excitement and pleasant anticipation, with our hearts only half in our work. The phone rang—one long, one short, our ring—and I raced to answer it.

"Let me speak to your father," a man's voice said.

So Papa went to the phone, engaging in a maddeningly unsatisfactory conversation. "Yes—no—yes—no—yes. I'll come right in."

"The General—?" Mama asked, once the receiver was back in place.

Papa nodded.

"Sick?" Mama asked. Her voice trailed off. "Or—or something—?"

"In the calaboose. Ben Hudson called."

Ben Hudson was the justice of the peace, but so seldom were his services required that we sort of forgot about him.

"Ben Hudson—" Mama said. "What does he expect you to do?" After all, it was his job to handle matters like this.

"He said I could bring him home, if I wanted to come for him."

"What was wrong?" Mama asked.

"Drunk," Papa told her.

Now that was something. The preacher talked against it, and the chart at school showed, in such vivid illustrations I couldn't bear to examine the gory things, what liquor did to your insides. Besides, Mama belonged to the W.C.T.U., and what would people think if she had Someone Who Drank about the house?

"Go get him," Mama said firmly, while our chins dropped down on our breastbones. Honestly, there was just no way of telling what parents would do next.

So we missed Sunday school, making the occasion truly world-shaking in its gravity. Finally Papa drove into the driveway. Yes, The General sat beside him. Now we would get a firsthand version of the whole episode, about the nature of which, until now, we knew little or nothing. Anyway, that's what we thought. We reckoned without Mama.

"Get away from that window," she ordered.

We drew away, prepared to protest. But an even sterner dictum was in wait for us.

"And go outside and play," Mama continued. "You're not to be in the kitchen when he comes in."

"But Mama—" I was not one to give in without argument.

"I said—go *outside*. And take the others with you."

Given to argument I might be, but I still recognized the voice of authority when I heard it. So I led Brother and Sister out into the front yard. Then, threatening them with all sorts of vengeance if they followed, I slipped back to the front porch, placing myself at the opened door so that I could see straight down the hall which ran through the house to the kitchen. It was like having a box seat at the theater, and what I saw was as moving as any good play.

The General was trembling all over, like a sick man. When he came in the back door his head was down and he hesitated for a moment. Then he looked straight at Mama, the way a Christian probably acted when he faced the lions in that last hopeless minute. He marched straight to her, and once there, he made his bow.

"Lady," he said, "I am ashamed. I went into the local pub (what a name for the little saloon), and once in there, began to talk politics. I let myself get out of control—" He stood a little straighter. "I will leave, if you wish me to. I only came back for my clothes."

"Nonsense," Mama said. "We all make mistakes now and then. There's a kettle of hot water on the stove in the basement. Take a bath and change clothes. By that time I'll have your tea ready. Only," and how she was to know this I've often wondered since, "I expect coffee would really be better."

And coffee it was, later, when The General was once more clean and respectable. With it Mama served ham and eggs and strawberry preserves, just as she would have done to any welcome and honored guest. We children were allowed in the room (with strict orders ahead of time not to say so much as a single word about what had happened), and things went on as in any ordinary meal. Papa even ate some more, just to be sociable, and we children, always ready for food, wolfed bread and preserves. After all, it had been a good three hours since breakfast.

So far as I know, the incident was never mentioned afterward. The General went to "the village" no more, except for necessary supplies, and then with Papa, coming home when he did. In the fall, he drifted on. His farewell to Mama was a scene which still stands out in my mind. He stood before her, hat in hand, his thin gray hair neatly parted, his old blue eyes misted over.

"You are not only a great Lady," he said. "You are a good woman as well. The two are not always synonymous."

(I went to the dictionary as soon as he was gone, and promptly added a new word to my vocabulary.)

"Thank you," Mama said, making no disclaiming, taking the compliment as sincerely as it had been given. "Good luck to you. Drop us a note sometime, if you feel like it."

She knew he wouldn't, but it made her farewell warm and

personal, as if a friend were leaving for a temporary absence. Actually, The General was passing out of our lives, and we'd never hear of him again.

As a matter of fact, we did, but in a way we could not have foreseen. One evening nearly two years later Papa was reading the Kansas City *Star*.

"Here," he said, passing the paper across to Mama, "what do you make of this?" He pointed to an item he had just read.

Mama read it and was quiet for a long time. Finally she spoke.

"It's the same, of that I'm sure," she said.

Then she read it to us.

The item concerned an old man, believed to be William T. Cunningham, an Englishman, who had been found dead in Chicago. "Judging from papers found on his person, it is thought that he was a member of a family of some consequence in England."

"That was his name," Papa said. "It sounds like him."

"Poor old thing," Mama said. "No one to care—"

In that, she was wrong. All at once Sister and I began to cry, tears streaking down our cheeks so fast we could scarcely mop them up. I think The General would have been pleased. Not at our tears—never that. But he would have been proud to know that in a Missouri farm kitchen, two little girls mourned for him. He was not alone in the world.

Somewhere down the line, the order of his coming not clear in our minds, Lije arrived. When Papa brought him home, Mama said, "Well, you've been stung this time, all right. I've always told you it would happen, giving a job to the first one who came asking for it."

"Wait and see," was all Papa had to say.

I was about eleven at the time, and not overly large for my age. Lije was scarcely an inch taller than I was.

"You'll be taller when you grow up," Sister encouraged him the first evening.

"I'm thirty-five," he told her.

"Golly—" Brother said.

So we knew for sure Mama was right. No grown man as small

as that could be of any great use around the farm. Milk, maybe, and feed the stock and run errands. But real work was another thing.

We couldn't have been more wrong. Lije might be little but he had steel for muscles and he went after work the way a terrier dug out a rat. The best thing about him, however, was the knack he had for handling horses, a skill which recommended him to Papa, who would have no man about the place if he abused animals.

"Lije talks to horses," Brother reported solemnly. "And they understand every word he says."

"Oh, come on now," we scoffed.

Sister and I hung around, seeking evidence to disprove so improbable a statement. Finally we had to admit, reluctantly, that Brother might be right. Horses did seem to understand whatever he said to them. Finally we came right out and asked Lije about it.

"Well," he admitted, "I suppose you could say I have a way with horses. It's because I used to be a jockey."

Now that *was* something. Every Missouri child knew about horse racing. We were witness to this thrilling sport at any kind of celebration from the local street fair on up to the state fair at Sedalia. We asked, practically, why he had quit so enchanting a business.

"I got too heavy," he explained mournfully.

Too heavy! Our eyes bulged. Lije, too heavy?

"They kept me down to a hundred and ten for a year," he told us, "by making me stay on a diet and having me sit over tubs of hot water every night, trying to sweat the pounds off. But when a man gets past thirty, he gains weight in spite of all he can do."

"Tell us about it," we begged, "—the races, we mean."

"I rode in the Kentucky Derby," he said.

We knew about that, and pressed for details, which he gave.

"And once on Epsom Downs," he went on, plainly inspired by our interest.

My only association there was with certain small white

crystals which Mama occasionally mixed, with water, into a nauseous concoction I took under threat of being spanked if I refused. I must have shown my lack of interest.

"That's in England," he said. "Except there, they call it the 'Darby.' Three-year-olds, they run."

Now that was something.

"Once the King and Queen were there when I rode."

"Oh," I cried, "what did the Queen look like?"

"I don't know, miss," Lije told me. "I had to keep my eye on my horse."

That was Lije, all right. Not even a queen could tempt him to look away from his horse.

They came and they went, those hired men. I do not believe we have their likes in these days, although I, sitting in my house on its sixty-foot lot, would really have no way of knowing. I am sure, as I look back, that I remember mostly the good ones. Papa must have brought home a lemon now and then. A few I recall vaguely—the one who beat the horses and used Such Language that Papa had to fire him on the spot; the young city fellow who minced around for a week and decided, after the Cow With the Horns cornered him in the lot and held him there until Papa went down and took the matter in hand, that he was "too good for farm work"; the poor youth who came down with appendicitis the first day and had to be shipped off to a hospital; and many colorless ones who had nothing to recommend them save that they were good workers.

But we children always hoped for the best. In fact, Sister and I were quite big girls, ready for high school and doing our hair up on curlers every night, before we quit staring, round-eyed, at the hired men Papa brought home with him.

And I think that even now, if the years should roll back and we could all be home about that time of year—which of course, is impossible—my heart would give a faint remembering flip if Papa came home to announce, "Well, I hired a man today."

II.

Hello, Central

THE hired man might well be your bulwark against disaster on the farm, your dispenser of news and your bard from the great world beyond, but in matters touching the larger, more general—and certainly more important—welfare and for an information center, we turned to Central as automatically as a flower turns to the sun and with the same confident expectation that our needs would be fulfilled. For example, there was the night the Borden house caught on fire.

It so happened that the fire was in April, and came because a faulty brooder blazed up, taking the lives of a hundred baby chickens and, for a while, threatening the house itself. It could just as easily have started at some other season of the year and for a number of other reasons. But the action Sarah Borden took, upon making the discovery, would have been the same no matter when or where it started.

She called Central.

She was alone when it happened, at ten o'clock at night, and afterward, when the rich details went humming along the telephone lines, the invariable question was, "Oh, Sarah, whatever did you do when you found out the house was on fire?"

"Well," Sarah answered, "first I called Central and then I started praying."

Nobody considered the answer sacrilegious. That was the standard order in which we handled our emergencies. Nor was it an order without justification. God was undoubtedly the center of the universe, but Central was what her name implied—the focal point of the community. Besides that (a theory never admitted, just acted upon), we could probably get to her a lot quicker and may have called upon her more often. And, secretly, we even suspected her of knowing more about us.

This was a supposition not without justification. She knew our business better than we did ourselves because hers was a three-dimensional knowledge not only gleaned from our version of things but likewise supplemented by that of our friends and kin, plus a generous dash of information volunteered by our enemies. Piecing these bits of information together she often came up with a solution that might well have baffled Scotland Yard.

For instance, the night the Borden house caught fire, Sarah screamed, "Help! Central! Fire!" into Central's ears and then hung up the receiver without giving her name. Central didn't have time to waste in verifying the source of the call. Immediately she plugged in on the six hundred line, the origination of the call, and rang eight longs, the signal that a general announcement was about to be made. She listened to the sound of receivers coming off the hook, like the patter of hail on a tin roof, until she judged she had enough farmers listening and then she told them about their neighbor's plight.

"How did you know where the fire was if Sarah didn't tell you?" someone asked curiously.

"Easy enough. Sarah Borden is the only woman on the six hundred line who lisps."

The eight longs—signal for a general announcement—was a sound familiar to my childhood. Mama, if she were busy, would delegate me to tune in, in order to get the information.

"Now listen," she would admonish me. "Be sure you get it straight."

It might be an advertisement for specials on groceries, a free picture show sponsored by the local merchants, the ice cream social given by the Church, a circus coming to town, the community picnic or even, as was the case in the Borden fire, some emergency which bespoke the help of the neighborhood. Fortunately this latter case was rare. More often Central was called upon to dispense a vast store of general knowledge. She was considered by the community as an animated encyclopedia, a dictionary, a living newssheet, and a trouble shooter. Between intervals of getting numbers called for, she would be kept busy answering questions like these:

Central, what's burning? I see a fire in the West.
Central, what's on at the show tonight?
Central, who died? I hear the bell tolling.
Central, would you know how long to cook apple jelly?
Central, what time is it? My clock's stopped.
Central, how is Grandpa Williams this morning?
Central, how do you spell "and-so-forth"?

That's a sample taken at random from an ordinary, routine morning. At such times as the information was pertinent, she would be called upon to give the result of the school board election, tell whether last night's frost was supposed to have hurt the fruit, and give the location of Mr. Halsted's threshing machine.

Not only would Central answer all these questions, with a high degree of accuracy and some personal admonitions thrown in, but she would also obligingly give bulletins on the sick, quoting such details as temperature, appetite (or lack of it), and the way the patient had (or hadn't) rested last night. She knew if the doctor was going to call, and if any out-of-town kin had either arrived or planned to do so.

"I'll just call Central," Mama would say, "and ask her how Mrs. Desmond is this morning. No need to bother the family, with all they have to do at a time like this."

And, if the worst happened, Central was a clearing house for all the details pertinent to the funeral arrangements, such as hour of services, pallbearers, minister in charge, and flowers ordered from out-of-town florists.

In that same vein, she was also an authority on train and bus schedules, even for lines some distance away. This information she traded with other operators in a kind of freemasonry arrangement.

In those days, a telephone call was a deeply satisfying experience, a time for utter relaxation on your part. Once you whirred that little crank on the side of the phone, your chore was finished. You didn't even have to know the number you were calling. Central kept them all in her head.

"Hello, Central," Mama would say, "I want to talk to Sister Katherine." Or, "Give me my mother." Or, "Ring Mrs. Bessie Williams."

I honestly think Central would have been a little hurt had we asked for our party by number, considering this as an indication we did not trust her. Or, she probably would have taken us for Somebody From Away From Here, who had not yet got in tune with the community. Her knowledge was even more personal than that. She knew if Sister Katherine, or whoever it was you were calling, was temporarily out of the house.

"She's not at home," Central would report. "I heard her say she was going over to Mrs. Beckman's. Want me to call her there?"

Central Office was located on Main Street, housed in a building with a plate-glass front. Central, sitting on her high stool at the switchboard, had a look-in on the comings and goings of the whole community. She lived in a fishbowl-in-reverse world. Mostly she had only to raise her eyes to know the whereabouts of anyone who happened to be in town at the moment. Women at home, caught in some emergency, would call Central to see if she could help in locating a husband, child, or friend to whom it was necessary to deliver a message.

"Hello, Central. Do you see Frank Hardin anywhere on the street? If you do, tell him to get some sugar. I'm out, and I need it to make a cake."

"Central, is Bill around somewhere? Tell him Cousin Mamie Bledsoe just drove in from California and wants to see him."

Usually Central could, and did, put her finger on the person wanted almost immediately.

These days, in order to make a long-distance call, one has to memorize a string of numerals reminiscent of the size of the national debt. Then, you left it all to Central. You simply said "Central, I want to talk to my brother, Sam Mitchell, in Kansas City."

She didn't ask if you had his number, area code, extension, and all the rest of it. She didn't ask his street address or initials. She did, however, probably want to know if anything was wrong, and express the hope that nobody was sick and that you didn't have any bad news. A long-distance call was an occasion in those days. Anybody who made one was slightly nervous before, during, and after it. You were relieved to have Central standing between you and any unpleasantness which might occur. And the way she did talk up to that other operator—

"Now listen, Kansas City—my party can't hear. You give us another connection. And don't start charging until he can really talk."

Plainly you had a friend at court, and she'd make things go right or know the reason why. It seems to me we never could hear. Not well, that is. Occasionally Central had to take drastic measures.

"Now listen to me," she'd call darkly. "All you people on the seven hundred line hang up your receivers. You just weaken the circuit, having them down."

More often than not the soft, muffled clicking of receivers going up would be heard. Of course, there were always a few who refused to co-operate. Rugged individualists, these, convinced they had a right to take down their own receiver if they wanted to, and nobody was going to tell them to hang it up.

Mama was, on the whole, pretty high-minded about eavesdropping. Mostly, she didn't. Usually we waited for our ring—a long and a short—before we went to the phone, although, of course, there were exceptions, as when a neighbor was sick or in some sort of difficulty. Then it was plainly our duty to listen rather than to bother the family with a call of our own. Not everyone was so careful.

I recall going to see a neighbor one afternoon—not close

friends of ours, but still somebody Mama felt the need to call on. There was a largish family—five or six girls whose ages ranged from ten to twenty. Scarcely were we seated than the phone rang—two longs, two shorts.

"You get it, Mabel," the mother said.

"But that's not your—" I began and got stopped in mid-sentence by a Look from Mama.

Mabel went, obediently, stood at the phone (most phones were on the wall those days, so one stood up to talk. I recall that everyone thought Mama was given herself airs when she had ours put low enough that she could sit down while talking), and by and by came back to report.

"That was Mrs. Hicklin calling Mrs. Finch. She said her eggs weren't hatching."

"Lands sakes," her mother said.

Three times while we were there the episode was repeated, with a different girl covering the call each time. They seemed to have it worked out according to some system understood, and honored, by all.

"My goodness, Mama," I marveled on our way home. "Did you notice? They listen to everybody—all the time. I guess they listen to you, too."

"Of course," Mama said unconcernedly. "At least, now I know whose clock it is I hear ticking every time I talk."

I don't believe anybody ever objected. Like Caesar's wife, your telephone conversation was supposed to be blameless. And anyway, you couldn't have stopped the eavesdropping had you wanted to. Besides, if you were anything like clever, you learned "to have signals agreed on ahead of time . . ." cryptic little half-statements, family jokes meaningful only to the ones speaking. I have heard Mama and her sisters carry on a fifteen-minute conversation with not one sentence meaning exactly what it seemed to say. By the time somebody on the line figured she had the talk decoded, they would have changed all the signals, and the eavesdropper would be left just where she started out —knowing those two women were pulling a fast one over her.

Central herself could be master of the half-truth, the evasive answer if occasion seemed to warrant. It happened the time Laura Keith was trying to locate her husband, Dick.

We said Laura was a nagger and we said Dick was henpecked, and to the last one of us, our sympathy went out to him. At the precise moment Laura was trying to locate him, he was sitting on a bench in front of the Central office, enjoying a good talk with Bud Malone, his friend and comforter. He had only settled down five minutes before. A man ought to have a longer recess than that. Even children at school got more.

"Central," Laura Keith's voice clanged (she did sound exactly like a fire engine bell, a lot of people said), "—Central, do you see Dick Keith anywhere? If you do, tell him to come home right away. Pet is choking to death."

Central turned her head away from the window.

"No," she said smoothly, "I don't see him."

Afterward, she justified herself. "That Pet is beyond a doubt the most worthless dog in town. She *ought* to choke to death."

"Besides," she added, after a moment's thought, "I had my head turned and I *really* didn't see him."

It was a great comfort to us, living in rural homes, to know that we had Central to call upon. Storms could, and did, sweep over us. Roads might be blocked with snow, bridges washed out, great trees thrown across the road by last night's wind. Central couldn't prevent these disasters, of course, but she could keep us informed about them and, upon occasion, give us help in circumventing nature.

I remember one winter's night waking to the sound of confusion and excitement. I went down, shivering in my nightgown, arriving just in time to see Papa, all muffled up in his overcoat and boots and cap, going outside. He gave a good sound knock on the door of the hired man's room and was, in a moment, joined by him.

"Little Tim Houston's sick," Mama said. "Central called to say Dr. Carney was on his way, but there might be a snowdrift just this side of Houston's."

Central knew where Dr. Carney was—delivering the Stevens baby—because she was the one who invented the answering service. It would never have occurred to the good doctor to go anywhere without first alerting her. So naturally when Mrs. Houston screamed into the transmitter, "Tim's dying," Central could take over with not a moment wasted.

Of course, Tim's illness came at a most inconvenient time—midnight, and Dr. Carney dead tired from getting the baby into the world. The Houstons were like that—given to emergencies at the wrong times. Still, it was fortunate that Dr. Carney was in their general direction, so it was easy enough to call him and give him the information. Luckily the baby was already there and things were going smoothly, so he could leave. It was not until he had hung up that Central remembered about the possibility of the snowdrifts and decided she had better get Papa and the other neighbors on the job. She made only one slip. So occupied was she with organizing things that she had forgotten to ask whether the new baby was a girl, a boy, or twins. People were going to be disappointed when they called to ask in the morning.

Dr. Carney pulled Tim through and he grew up to be a responsible citizen. He had to—any number of people, including Central herself, were not above reminding him of all the trouble they had taken for his sake one cold January night. In a way, they dared him to come to any bad end.

We all used the relaying service offered by Central. Not only did she have sure knowledge of Dr. Carney's comings and goings, but she could also keep in mind the whereabouts of half-a-dozen people who were expecting calls. It was a common occurrence to say, "Central, I'll be at Cousin Belle's for the next hour. If anybody calls, ring me there." She would even take over entirely in case of death or grave illness or other emergency, provided she was asked to do so, telling callers the home was not receiving calls just now but that she, Central, would be glad to take the message and pass it on.

She could be the guardian of happy occasions as well.

An uncle and an aunt were celebrating their golden wedding. A son came home, but the daughter-in-law was unable to attend.

The day before the celebration, the daughter-in-law decided to telephone from Florida, just so she could be a part of the big doings. The call came through at the time the principals in the great affair were downtown. The son answered the home phone, explaining it was too bad but his mother and father were not in. At that moment Central, who knew exactly what was going on (people didn't call long distance from Florida just to chat with people they could talk to any time) broke in:

"Now just be quiet a minute," she told the son. "I have your folks on the line."

And so she did—one of them in the office's single pay-booth, the other at the switchboard, headphone on ears.

For five minutes all telephone service in our little Missouri community was held up while a four-way conversation went on among a daughter-in-law in Florida, a son on the home phone, and the celebrating couple in the Central office.

So far as I ever heard, no one saw fit to complain about this temporary suspension of service. Doubtless, however, if complaint had come, Central would have hushed it by saying that, in her opinion, fifty years of happy married life should very well rate five minutes of silent tribute by the community.

Actually, there were at least three Centrals, sometimes more, each serving a separate shift. But we merged them into one personality, bearing a single name and possessing a common trait, a dedication to our interests. Even the youngest knew this. I am told that once I fell and hurt myself and, even as I rose up from my prone position, I screamed, "Call Central and ask her what to do with this cut!"

You had to be a little more grown-up to rate a service which, I think, was unique with our own Central. Given occasionally during the week, it came to its full flower on Saturday. About five o'clock on that afternoon one could see boys and young men slipping into Central Office, singly, and in small groups. They went in looking a little embarrassed and self-conscious, and, more often than not, they came out looking pleased with themselves and the world.

They had gone to ask Central which girls did not have dates

for the evening. By and large, that was the era before Going Steady, and Saturday night dates were catch-as-catch-can. This was information concerning which Central had complete and thorough knowledge, for she had already put through the calls. Now she passed on the facts, with no feeling of embarrassment on either her part or that of the inquiring youths. There wasn't any sense of calling a girl who already had a date—and just tying up the line that long, only to be turned down. On the other hand, there wasn't any excuse for a girl sitting at home and doing nothing when there was a boy who wanted to take a girl out for the evening. It was an eminently sensible arrangement, one approved by everyone in the community.

It is not yet easy for me to realize that with Direct Distance Dialing, the whole responsibility of getting a long-distance call through is right on my shoulders. If, in my excitement, I place a finger in the wrong digit, a supercilious female voice (recorded, and as impersonal as the wind blowing) tells me I've just committed a boo-boo and I'd best hang up and try again. She doesn't even say, "Better luck this time." Central never did it like that.

For example, there was the day when a woman's desperate voice came in over long distance from a town a good hundred miles away.

"Listen, Central," the woman said, "I have to get hold of my husband right away. I'm going to have a baby."

Babies were no problem to rural Centrals. They knew better than did his own family where to locate the doctor. But this woman wanted her husband, which was not unusual either.

"Who is your husband?" Central asked.

"Boyd Jones."

The town had several Joneses, but none named Boyd. Besides, this was long distance, so the man was not a native.

"Do you know for sure he's in this community."

"Yes—he's working there."

"Who's he working for?"

"I can't tell you. I lost the letter with the man's name in it."

Now that was a problem, even for Central.

"I want him right away," the woman said, a thin edge of hysteria frazzling the edges of her voice.

Probably her first baby, and she's scared, Central thought. "Now don't get excited. Can you tell me what the man he works for does?"

"I don't know. He just got the job. But he said the man had a Dodge truck."

So did several other men in the community. Of course, she could go down the list, asking. But it would be better if she could put the call through right now, with the woman so excited and scared and all.

"And he lives next door to a man who owns a mean German police dog, and no fence around his house. But *he's* got a fence."

"Oh—"

And with this relevant bit of information, Central was able to get Boyd Jones on the line in less than five minutes. He had just come to work for Milt Harmon, who owned a transfer business and had a Dodge truck and lived next door to Hal Jameson who had a German police dog everybody in town thought ought to be fenced in.

Certainly I wouldn't go so far as to say that modern phones aren't miracles of technology and convenience. I can dial almost anyone I might wish to talk to in the United States or Canada. And, doubtless, in a few years I can do the same thing by bouncing a message off Telstar and so communicate with friends in Siberia and Uganda and—who knows—Venus and the Moon. But it's not quite the same.

Central was the living, breathing, knowledgeable heart and mind of the community. Man has not yet become smart enough to make a gadget which will replace a heart or a mind.

Nor is he apt to do it.

III.

Not a Speck of Dirt

A S I remember, it usually started in March, and although I am not sure she ever knew her part in it, Central—or, more properly, the telephone—set the ritual in motion.

House cleaning, that was.

Mrs. Lindstrom was the one who took the initiative. She had an instinct about the matter, a built-in radar which told her the warm spell was for real and not just a weather breeder to be followed by cold rains and maybe even snow, a condition which frequently trapped the unwary or the novitiate at the house-keeping business. Mama insisted that Mrs. Lindstrom got up one fine morning, stuck her nose out the kitchen door and tested, as one did, with a finger to determine the wind's direction. Having done this, she knew exactly when the time was right to start reaming out the house. (Papa suggested that maybe it was an instinct similar to the one which told the groundhog whether to come out or go back for another six weeks. But we knew he was joking, because he didn't at all believe in that groundhog stuff.)

No sooner was Mrs. Lindstrom well started than word went over the country line. Central might just as well have rung eight longs and made the general announcement.

"Mrs. Lindstrom began house cleaning today."

"She did—uhm-um-um—"

Before the hour was up, all up and down the countryside rugs would be flapping on clotheslines, curtains tossing about in washing machines, and contents of dresser drawers dumped upon floors.

The Big Push was on.

Of course, no one could hope to come up to Mrs. Lindstrom's performance, for she was easily the best housekeeper in the community, perhaps, some contended, in the county or even the state. It was said she washed down the outside of her house twice yearly. Some claimed she scrubbed the roof, although there was no record of anyone's actually having seen her do this. The story got itself into the folklore of the community, however, and I for one would never try to disprove it. They said she washed, starched, and ironed her curtains every other month. They said she washed her dishes so vigorously that all the flowers wore off. They said she made her husband take off his shoes before he walked inside the door. They said she washed every vegetable they ate with soap and water and then rinsed them three times.

It was her own proud boast that she disinfected the door knobs and the outdoor john every week. Her one comment, when Papa had a bathroom put in at our house, was a brief and succinct remark about johns inside houses, couched in good earthy Anglo-Saxon words.

I remember once when I went on an errand for Mama I found her busy with a pan of soapy water washing out the transmitter of the telephone.

"When you come to think of it," she said, "there's nothing gets any dirtier than the mouthpiece of a telephone. People all the time breathing into it."

Scrub, scrub, scrub she went while I sat there remembering guiltily the time I had used her telephone more than a year ago, thus contributing to the store of germs she was now demolishing. However, she had probably scrubbed several times since then, so I did not hold myself too responsible.

Nowadays she'd probably be a candidate for the psychiatrist's couch. Then, she was an Example. Although no woman could hope to come up to her, they all tried, after their fashion, to emulate her. Perhaps, after all, she wasn't entirely responsible for the frenzy of cleaning which struck our community come spring. Perhaps it was an event which came of itself, when the season was right—as dandelions and strawberries and new potatoes; as inevitable as small boys playing marbles and then, for no apparent reason, shifting to baseball.

At our house—and in other homes I suspect, although I wouldn't know for sure—there was a well-established order to the house cleaning, with everyone knowing his own part in the undertaking. While hired girls were by no means as inevitable with us as were hired men, still we often had one, especially at this time. Together she and Mama started in an upstairs bedroom and worked down. Of course all rugs must be taken off the floors and hung over the clothesline to be beaten. No manufacturer makes rugs like that any more. This beating was no half-hearted, once-over-lightly business. The boys in the family were given a sort of flail, an instrument patterned after the implements used by ancient peoples to beat grain out of the straw. Thus armed, they set to work with more alacrity than one would expect. Slamming doors was, of course, forbidden; if you vented your ill-temper in this manner you would be sent back to close the door again. Softly, this time. But you could work your mad out on a rug and your mama would beam at you.

Curtains came down, leaving the room looking curiously naked and defenseless. There were two schools of thought concerning beds. Mrs. Lindstrom, of course, dismantled hers, taking every slat, the springs and mattress, and the bed itself outside for a scrubbing with carbolic acid in the scrub water. Mama compromised by taking the mattress out for a good airing and using the broom on the slats and springs. Mama was an adequate, not a dedicated, housekeeper. But everyone, regardless of her persuasion, hung feather pillows on the line to sun, and washed the quilts and comforts and blankets. From all the fuss about the bedclothes, you would have thought that every single one of us had gone to bed every night wearing muddy shoes.

Cleaning closets and drawers could be, and often was, a rewarding process. Usually this resulted in the dredging up of treasures lost all winter.

"So that's where your overshoes were—"

(I, especially, was given to losing things. Three pairs of over-shoes to the season was about par for me. Count one for home, one to be inevitably left at school, and one to be found in some out-of-the-way spot come spring cleaning.)

Mama also found things you wished had remained lost. Like dresses that were too short for me but not yet quite the right size for Sister. Mama got a Certain Light in her eyes when she looked at one of these.

"Perfectly good," she'd say. "All it needs is a little letting out."

The only trouble was that the "letting out" exposed a portion a good two shades darker than the rest of the dress. I stormed and vowed I'd never wear that awful thing. It made me look like a freak.

But, I wore it.

Such cleaning out sometimes brought incriminating things to light, like the half-finished Christmas note which should have been sent to Cousin Mittie no later than mid-January.

"But honestly, Mama, I thought I had—"

It was dreadful, writing a thank-you note in March. I mean, what can you say about a handkerchief you lost in February, or a book you finished Christmas week and didn't like anyway.

There were also apple cores stuffed back into the darkest corner of the closet and candy wrappers you had meant to clean up, sure as anything, the next morning after you smuggled the contraband delicacies to bed with you.

House cleaning was like the Last Judgment. Your sins popped up and found you out.

Ordinarily house cleaning was a woman's business, like the Ladies Aid, and men kept out of it, but I remember one time when Papa took over. It was in the matter of scrubbing the kitchen.

This was a huge room, large enough to accomodate any number of pieces of furniture, including two stoves. One, a coal-burning range, was used in cold weather. The other, smaller stove, used in summer but remaining in the kitchen all the time, varied with the years. The earliest version I remember used carbide gas, the same fuel which gave us our lights. It was generated in a large tank buried in the ground just back of the summer kitchen. Later, when Papa had electricity installed, we had an electric range.

Besides the stoves, there was a table which, when the leaves were raised, could seat eight. There were, of course, chairs to accommodate that many people; a sink, a kitchen cabinet, a dish cupboard and one for cooking utensils, a rocking chair; and, naturally, room enough for people to sit around and watch while the meal was being prepared. It was, in short, a proper Missouri kitchen.

Wainscotting, painted cream, extended up for about three feet; the walls and ceiling were light blue.

"It needs scrubbing," Mama announced.

"Wouldn't it be better to paint?" Papa asked, surveying the vast expanse that was the kitchen.

"Nonsense," Mama said. "Just think how much cheaper it will be to scrub. Mrs. Lindstrom always does."

"Oh, that one—" Papa said expressively.

"The first day it's too wet for Mert to work (that was our current hired man) we'll all start scrubbing."

Came a rainy day.

"Fine," Mama exulted. "Dirt comes off easier in this kind of weather."

So she herded us all to the kitchen, with soap and rags and pails and brushes. Like an experienced general, she deployed her troops according to their various abilities. Sister and I were assigned the wainscotting. Mama would take the lower half of the walls, Papa the parts she couldn't reach. Mert, on a stepladder, was assigned the ceiling.

You'd think, with so great a company of workers, there would have been a space problem. Not in our kitchen. The furniture, except the stoves and cabinets, was moved out, and we all fell to with a reasonable amount of enthusiasm. All except Mert, that is.

His was a distaste entirely justified. In order to scrub a ceiling properly, one must use plenty of soap and water. The law of gravity takes over. Soapy water runs down the worker's arm, down the shoulder, down to the waist. If you look up, it splats you in the face; if you don't look up, you miss spots and leave streaks.

"Isn't this fun!" Mama chirped. "Just see how nice it is, where you've scrubbed.'"

Brother didn't scrub. His duty was to stand in the middle of the floor and call our attention to places we had missed. He was enjoying himself hugely. I am surprised the experience didn't put its mark on him and make him grow up to be a section boss.

"You've missed a streak right there to the left, Mert," Brother said in reproving tones.

Bang—down went Mert's bucket of scrub water, right into the middle of the kitchen floor, narrowly missing the young straw boss.

Thud, thud—Mert's feet hit the rungs of the stepladder.

"—— —— —— ——" Mert yelled. "I'm not going to stand up on this blankety-blank ladder scrubbing anybody's blankety-blank ceiling. I ain't going to be bossed by no blankety-blank brat. I'm quitting."

He stalked out of the kitchen, leaving a wet slushy trail behind him.

We stared dumbly at each other. Not that we minded losing Mert, personally. He was glum and, so far as we had ever been able to discover, had never known one interesting experience. Still, it was getting close to corn-planting time, and we had to have a hand.

Papa started after him.

"What are you going to do?" Mama asked. "Beg him to stay, after he talked That Way before the children?"

"Give him his pay," Papa said. "And then I'm going to town for Bill Schuster."

Mama's eyes were round. Bill was the local painter.

"What color do you want it painted?" Papa asked. "Same as before?"

"Same as before," Mama said meekly.

The next morning he did bring back Bill, with his stepladders and canvas and brushes, and the paint, in big gallon buckets. A tall wiry man, ageless and merry, helped carry the things in. He was the new hand, name of Sam. Brother, of course, told him why Mert had quit.

"Now isn't that a shame," Sam said. "I wouldn't have minded scrubbing detail at all. I've been to sea and swabbed down decks aplenty."

It took Bill Schuster the best part of a day to paint the kitchen. We had a picnic supper that evening, and the whole house smelled divinely of paint and turpentine. For days Mama found specks of it in our hair and on our clothes. As I remember, she didn't fuss overmuch. No normal child could be expected to stay out of the way while the painter was busy at his fascinating work.

Of course, we were very lucky to get Bill Schuster on such short notice. He was an artist in his way, temperamental and spoiled as all get-out. He was subject to spells of what he called painter's colic, so women always had extra good meals while he was working. It was almost like cooking for the Presiding Elder. In addition to the regular meals, he demanded a good lunch, morning and afternoon.

When Mama saw how nice the kitchen looked (and since it was all Papa's idea in the first place), she said Bill might as well do the whole downstairs, now that he was out here. We burned coal in the furnace, and Missouri coal is soft. We had ivory woodwork all over the house, and one swipe across it convinced Mama that it needed painting. Anyway, we had Bill here, and he was in a good humor, and she had already baked chickens and two cakes and made potato salad. She could easily feed him another day or two.

With that much done, we had no choice but to paper.

Nowadays it is called decorating, and one brings in professionals. Efficient they are, but they are also impersonal and dull as dishwater. Mr. Garsten was made of different stuff. A slow, deliberate man, he talked incessantly as he worked. Of course, this demanded an audience. Mama complained that nobody got anything done while he was there, but actually we had no choice. Once we tried Mr. Marlowe, who was quick as greased lightning, but never got the white edges covered where the strips of paper joined. Another time we even tried putting it on ourselves. The hired man fell off the scaffold and hurt his wrist, right in the middle of corn planting; we children tripped over a chair on the back porch where the paper was being cut and ruined two rolls; while our backs were turned the little dog Fleas consumed an unknown quantity of paste and was very sick all over the kitchen floor. Papa said, "Never again."

It was much easier, and cheaper in the long run, to have Mr. Garsten come in, although he did set down certain conditions and talked our heads off while he worked.

First of all, the pattern of the paper should be easy to match. This was an intricate matter, quite beyond my understanding. It seemed that a wallpaper with a large, decided pattern had to be cut just so. If not, the design went all crazy across the wall, like a rocket exploding. It was necessary to waste a lot of paper, getting the design to hit at just the right spot. Mr. Garsten was an authority on this tricky process and had even been known to refuse to hang paper which he deemed too difficult to match.

There were certain other prerequisites. We got up early the day he was coming because every stick of movable furniture had to be carried out of the room. The rug must be taken up, and neither curtains nor shades were left at the windows. Naturally, every picture came down. Then, since this was the days before commercial paste, Mama made it for him.

She did this, using the prayerful care reserved for angel food cakes and currant jelly. Not long ago I tried to tell someone about this process, only to be laughed at. But I know I am right. I remember exactly how Mama made the paste Mr. Garsten used to put the paper on our walls. The proportions may have escaped me, but the method, never.

She took flour and mixed it into a thick paste with cold water. This done, she carried a tea kettle of boiling water to the paste and began pouring it in, slowly, while I stirred the concoction. She did this with the intense concentration of an Englishwoman making tea. None of us dared speak while she was at it. I stirred as if my very life depended upon my diligence. As soon as the water was out of the kettle, I lost my job. Mama took over, stirring vigorously until, at last, the paste was to her liking.

"Take it to Mr. Garsten," she would say to Papa when this degree of perfection was reached. She didn't dare go in herself— what if he found it lacking in some manner she could only surmise. She stayed in the kitchen until she heard his, "Exactly right," and then went in to watch.

Mr. Garsten had set up his wooden supports, which he called horses, and over them had spread several wooden planks. On this improvised table he had cut the paper, laying length on top of length. Now he took one of his brushes, spread the paste on the length of paper, doubled it over, and then walked to the wall with it. Here he had already set up a small platform which he climbed and put the top of the piece of paper to the wall. Slowly, surely, carefully he unfolded it and let it down. With a movement so deft and sure it was poetry to watch, he brought first a brush and then a length of cloth down the piece of paper. We watched, shivering in anticipation not unmixed with fear. What if it went on crooked! What if it didn't look as good on the wall as it did off! What if he tore a jagged bit in it! What if— The grim possibilities were almost without end, although all the time we knew our fears were groundless. Mr. Garsten never made a mistake.

And then, there it was on the wall. Exactly right. Straight as could be and without flaw. Lovelier than we had thought possible. Mr. Garsten was back at the working table once more. Slap, slap, slap, he dipped his wide brush into Mama's paste. Another piece of paper folded, lifted, attached to the wall. Matching the first one exactly. Not a smear of paste visible, not a white line showing. From his pocket he drew a small circular tool and cut off a small fraction at the bottom, just where the baseboard joined the wall. We relaxed; everything was going to be fine.

Of course, nobody could have torn himself away from such a completely fascinating process. Besides, Mr. Garsten worked better when he had an audience. He came forth with an endless stream of conversation, as effortless as it was entertaining. From the lips of a lesser man it might have passed for garrulousness or even plain gossip. Related by him, it became as entertaining as a weekly paper. For he talked not of his own knowledge but, after the fashion of the county paper, merely reported what had been told him by his daughter, Pansy.

Pansy read widely. She even, so Mr. Garsten maintained, read the Kansas City *Star* and *Times* from cover to cover every day, including the ads and the help wanted. Accordingly, he passed on to us wonderfully unrelated bits of information, as how many nails it took to build an average-sized house, where coal oil was first discovered, and what to do if bitten by a black widow spider. He was also an authority on the news of the community, for when Pansy was not reading she was, apparently, listening over the party line. He would relate to us some fascinating bit of information and then top it off with the by-line, as it were.

"Pansy was the first one that told me," he would assure us.

Finally, the last bit of paper was in place. Mr. Garsten would dismantle his table and scaffold; he would clean his brushes and ask us where we wanted the left-over paper stored. Once Papa had paid him, he would load his gear on a vehicle—not quite cart, not quite wagon—retrieve his horse from the stable where it had been feeding luxuriously all day, and make his way home where, doubtless, the waiting Pansy would restore him with food and information to fortify him against tomorrow's job.

And we were left with a room smelling of paste, damp like a cellar, and clean as a hospital operating room. He left us with more. To this good day, instead of saying "I told you so" we say, "Pansy was the first one that told you."

Mr. Garsten might be finished, but for us the work had barely begun. The rug would have to be brought back and placed on the floor which, of course, had been scrubbed. Then, naturally, the floor around the rug must be waxed, a process which was reserved for the very last of house cleaning. (Aunt

Margaret, always the one for finding a creative approach to whatever she did, devised a most happy solution for this floor waxing problem. She tied pieces of old blankets to her children's feet and let them have a skating party on the newly applied wax. They loved it!) Windows were washed and the curtains, nicely starched and ironed, were hung back at the windows. Shades were unrolled their full length and wiped with a slightly damp cloth. Furniture was cleaned and polished.

All the best dishes and the cut glass had to be washed and dried carefully. (It seems to me we put a dash of bluing into the rinse water for the glass, but I am not sure.)

Finally we were finished and everything was back in place. We walked softly, keeping our voices low, in a manner befitting the viewing of a miracle. Mama went to the phone to call a friend or some of the kin.

"Yes," she reported, smugness oozing out of her voice, "we're through. Not a speck of dirt anywhere."

As, indeed, there wasn't. Not for a few days, anyway. Before long we were once more practicing our accustomed, less frenetic brand of housekeeping. But the cleaning orgy had left its mark on us and, I am sure, for good.

There was this about house cleaning. It had a definite quality. You knew what you had to do and you knew when you had finished. It closed off one season, ushered in another, leaving you with a pleasant sense of accomplishment, clear-cut as getting promoted at school or graduating into the next size in dresses. More than that. It gave a sense of cleanness that went straight through you, not unlike the sensation which came from confessing to Mama that you hadn't really done the thing you said you would or, what was even more difficult, that you were guilty of something she could not have pinned on you had you not told her about it.

In short, it was an experience more effective than tranquilizers, a long sea voyage, or series of sessions with a psychiatrist.

And a great deal cheaper.

IV.

Friends of the Family

YOU had no time, really, to relax and enjoy your clean house because, in the natural course of events, about the time you were finished the chickens began to hatch.

The marvel to me now is that Mama ever got us to eat a bite of them, once they were out of the skillet.

Chickens were planned for so carefully before they were more than a germ in the egg, hung over so breathlessly while they were developing inside the shell, and guarded and nourished so assiduously once they were in the world that one would have thought they bore the status of close friends, if not actual kin, of the family. In spite of this, we made no protest when, a couple of months later, they appeared on the table—brown, crusty, utterly delicious. There is about children, I suppose, a certain callous matter-of-factness which accepts the inevitable and the natural destiny of things.

March came with the first warm days and a broody hen or two.

"Well," Mama would say, "might as well put a setting of eggs under each of them. Won't be any great loss if they walk off and leave the nest."

So she selected fifteen eggs, regular in shape, neither too small nor too large. (A neighbor boy once put a huge egg under a hen, and when it hatched, out popped *two* chickens joined by a single wing. The poor thing, or things, struggled about for a day or two until the boy's father mercifully put an end to the monstrosity, the boy howling in protest the while. Don't ever let anyone sell you a bill of goods about children being little darlings filled with love and compassion for all God's creatures, including their own kind, until they are taught hate by their elders. Children are, at heart, savages, possessed of a cruelty sometimes thoughtless, sometimes deliberate.)

Once you had selected eggs suitable for the purpose, you scratched a mark on one side with a pencil. The more imaginative used initials or even a design, but any old mark would do. Nature has thoughtfully put into brooding hens an instinct which causes them to turn, once each day, the eggs on which they are sitting. Failure to carry out this important chore will result in a lopsided chicken. Occasionally, however, a feckless hen will come along, probably all taken up with club work or maybe just bone-lazy, and neglect this necessary chore. It is a simple matter to pin her error on her for the unturned egg stands out boldly from the others. Then human hands can take over where Mother Nature went stale.

The goal was to have fried chicken for my birthday, which came early in June. I must confess this date was set not so much in my honor as it was to satisfy Mama's pride. There was considerable rivalry among the women to see who would be the first to slap a chicken into the skillet. This achievement was announced with complacency on the morning of the great event. Never the day before. One did not say, "I am going to have fried chicken tomorrow." As sure as you did a thing so naïve as that, some unscrupulous person was sure to go out that very evening, grab the biggest one in her flock and fry it for supper. No woman thus outsmarted would ever admit the chicken so sacrificed was really big enough. "She probably fried an egg," would be the acid comment on this tour de force.

Once Mama beat the date set for herself. Company came from Kansas City on Decoration Day, an occasion demanding special recognition. Mama went out and snatched up four chickens, one of them a pullet—a truly cardinal sin. She had Papa cut off their heads, we all fell to and picked them, and Mama dressed them. Of course, she barely had them in the skillet when she called to report the great event casually over the phone. Said the neighbor who received the tidings, "Did you carry them over from last year?"

Mama was never one to hold malice, but she probably went to her grave with that barb sticking in her soul.

I don't remember just when we bought an incubator and placed it in the basement. A mechanical hen, no less. A lamp was lighted at one end and in some way it sent the heat circulating through the trays of eggs, keeping them at the body temperature of a hen. Every morning those trays had to be pulled out and the eggs turned. We occasionally sprinkled them with water to counteract the drying effect of the artificial heat. I loathed the chore. I think I felt that I was rebelling against nature and that maybe the hens would parade in front of the basement door bearing "Unfair to Organized Henhood" on their biddy breasts.

There was, however, one advantage, and I would have been the first to admit it. Through the glass doors of the incubator we could witness, at close range, the tremendously thrilling sight of baby chicks popping out of their shells, stretching themselves, becoming living chickens. The miracle of birth unfolded before us. Watch a baby chicken getting itself out of the shell just once—the struggle, the final triumph—and you'll never lack respect for life again, be it human or animal.

In some mysterious way we always seemed to feel a little more responsible for incubator chickens. Perhaps we felt duty bound to make up to them for their orphan estate which we ourselves had brought upon them, even though they were almost immediately assigned to hen mothers who, after the first tentative efforts at "mothering up," accepted the waifs. Hens, however, are silly things at best and almost incapable of teaching their offspring, whether natural or the product of wooden boxes, the first principles of ordinary common sense. Not only do they panic at crossing a road; they don't have gumption enough to come in out of the rain. Chickens were always being led into watery deaths because their feckless mothers either couldn't or wouldn't conduct them to their own dry shelter when a storm came up.

As soon as the rain was over, we children were sent out into the dripping world to rescue such as were soaked or even chilled. These we brought into the kitchen for reviving. Usually warmth was enough to bring them around, but sometimes sterner measures were indicated. Long before I had ever heard of artificial respiration, I watched Mama as she picked up a limp chicken, opened its beak, and blew down its throat. Usually after the first few puffs it would give a feeble peep, then a convulsive shudder, and before long it was judged strong enough to join its brothers and sisters in a lined basket sitting on the oven door.

Of course, there were inevitable weaklings who couldn't make it. These were buried properly enough in a common grave, with no ceremony and no tears. That was one of the unbudgeable facts about chickens—you didn't expect to raise all you hatched.

Then, too, there were the occasional cripples and the odd ones which we children adopted as pets. One I remember especially. Through some unfortunate misalliance, or perhaps a quirk in heredity never fully understood, a white chicken hatched out of an egg supposedly laid by a proper Rhode Island Red hen. Naturally, the mother would not want to admit her indiscretion, if such there was, and equally of course, no other hen could be persuaded to adopt the freak. So we children undertook to raise it by hand.

We called it White Pet, and a great nuisance it came to be. The plain truth was that it never caught on it wasn't People. It wore doll dresses with a certain flair for style. When we grew weary of that, it chased grasshoppers and brought them to us, like a first-rate retriever. It also scooted into the house whenever the door was opened two inches, and was known to peck at visitors it found unacceptable. We would have as soon eaten a member of the family, so its natural destiny was closed to it. One day Mama, in desperation, sold it with a load of ordinary chickens. When we came home from school to find White Pet gone, our wails rent the heavens. But by and by we were consoled because, on the farm, there were always other pets to divert our minds.

For instance, there were two ducks, John and Julius. Never in animal or bird—and, I suspect, seldom in human—kingdom has there been such complete devotion as those two displayed for each other. Had Mama been the reader Papa was, she would doubtless have called them Damon and Pythias. Instead, she named them John and Julius after two devoted brothers she had known in her youth. For all we knew, they might more properly have been called Jane and Julia, but that was beside the point. The indisputable fact was their togetherness. Where one went, the other followed directly behind, keeping perfect formation, quack-quacking every step they took. Brother vowed they communicated with each other in a language which, had we been smart enough, we could have understood—where to find the juiciest insects, how best to evade watchful eyes and get into the lettuce bed, and weren't ducks smarter than tiresome people?

Finally Mama had enough of John and Julius marching about the yard. For goodness sakes, you can't have friends being met by those silly ducks, spat-spat-spatting under their feet, drowning out everyone's talking with their silly quacking. So she banished them from the yard to the nether regions bordering the pasture where the hogs were kept.

One day tragedy came. John—or maybe it was Julius—ventured into the enclosure where a particularly temperamental mother sow was guarding her newborn pigs. Naturally the inevitable happened. The sow, watchful for the welfare of her young—or maybe just a misanthrope of the animal world—objected loudly to the presence of the two visitors so close to her pen. Which stopped the two explorers not at all. They paused briefly on the fringe of danger, holding a clacking conference about their next move. One of them—we never were really sure which—had the edge on leadership, and now he seemed to be giving his brother a pep talk on the foolishness of fear. The other, apparently not convinced, still held back. Then, as if to demonstrate with action, the lead duck wriggled under the fence, into the pen.

Agonized squawks filled the air; the sow made short work of her visitor. And, even as we children added our wails to the confusion, we saw the other duck—John, or maybe Julius, depending on which one was now lying a limp mass of feathers inside the pen—follow, without a moment's hesitation, into the enclosure where his martyred brother lay. He surely knew the cause was hopeless and apparently chose the manner of his death. It wasn't long until there were two piles of white feathers there in the pen. But it was a long, long time before I really cared to sample pork again.

We had pigeons, which were great nuisances because they wanted to fly inside the house. There was, also, a gander which was satisfactory enough as a pet in his early years but became cantankerous with approaching age. "Mama," Brother would wail when he was small, "every time I go out in the yard he blows his nose at me." And finally, the hissing old meanie was sold.

Of course, not all our pets wore feathers. There were also cats. These were of two genre, barn cats and yard cats. The latter, of course, came into the house. The barn cats never ventured inside the yard fence. But, unknown to us, there must have been some fraternizing among the lot of them, for both groups had striking similarities.

We never thought of naming cats any more than we named the roses. There were the "climbing roses at the fences" and "the maiden blush at the edge of the garden." In like manner we designated our cats by their general characteristics—Mama Cat, the Big Tom Cat, Striped Kitty, White Foot, and so on. Some were better playfellows than others. We found them more satisfactory, by and large, than dolls for dressing up. True, they occasionally used their claws, but mostly we had it coming to us. They made up for this by being warm and cuddly as a real baby. Besides, they looked too convulsively cute when they took matters into their own paws and set off in awkward flight, still wearing dress and bonnet.

Once Papa bought us a couple of goats. I believe the idea was that they could be taught to draw a miniature farm wagon some implement company had sent as advertising. Free souls, the goats had no notion of becoming beasts of burden. Instead, they roamed about the place, making unmitigated nuisances of themselves. They chewed up everything in sight—harness, clothes flapping on the line, the upholstery in the new automobile.

And Mama had another complaint. "You just don't dare turn your back on them," she said.

Which, of course, you didn't.

Somehow, in spite of all this, we delayed ridding ourselves of them. Perhaps it was a busy season; maybe they were interesting enough that we really liked having them around; there might have been a certain hesitation, since we knew what their ultimate destiny would be, once they were sold; or, what is more likely, there just wasn't a market for goats in our part of the country. Anyway, they stayed on, scaring the living daylights out of the silly chickens, teasing the hogs but having cunning enough to remain on their own side of the tight fence. Then one day, they brought about their own undoing.

Mama had a sideboard in the dining room covered, after the fashion of the day, with choice specimens of cut glass. All women displayed this coveted item with downright ostentation. The dining room table (round, and big enough, when extended with "leaves," to seat maybe twenty people) also had its complement of glittering decorations, sitting exactly in the center, resting on an embroidered centerpiece. One day Mama walked into the dining room and saw a sight fit to paralyze the most intrepid woman.

On the sideboard, tiny hooves planted among the cut glass, stood one of the goats.

Mama had presence of mind enough to suppress the anguished scream which rose to her lips. The goat regarded her with calm and studied contempt, knowing well and good he had a despised human being completely at his mercy. Let her suffer, he seemed to say, as my kind have suffered down the ages at the hands of man. Head turned to one side he chewed rhythmically, his little beard moving up and down, up and down. Mama stood watching him, unable either to leave or to decide upon any constructive action.

It might have been five minutes, it might have been half an hour (Mama declared afterward it was a day and a half) that the two stood there in an earlier version of the Cold War. Neither budged. Except for the movement of the goat's beard, there was no motion on the part of either one of them. Then, either having had enough of the game or, perhaps, realizing he had made his point (certainly not moved by compassion), the goat jumped from the sideboard. Mama shut her eyes, waiting for the crash she knew was inevitable. No sound came, so by and by she opened them. Only a slit, but enough to see what was going on.

The goat stood on the dining room table, just to one side of the cut-glass bowl, his front feet planted firmly on the roses of the embroidered centerpiece. Then the war of nerves started all over again.

Mama lost count of time. Things were brought to a crisis by the slamming of the screen door on the back porch. Papa had come to the kitchen for a drink. The noise seemed to break the spell. Down jumped the goat from the table to the floor. At the same time, Mama was loosed from her horror. She laid on with the broom, and she laid on good. Papa was greeted as he stepped into the kitchen by the sight of the goat, for once set to flight, with Mama in hot pursuit, flailing away with the broom as if she were dispatching a rattlesnake.

"Well," Papa asked calmly, "you two playing a game? Which one's it?"

"You're going to sell that—that *Thing*," Mama gasped.

Papa thoughtfully opened the screen door just in time to let the goat sail out. It probably would have gone just as fast had he not done so.

"Now," he said, turning to Mama, "tell me—"

"You come look," Mama ordered.

Together they went to the dining room. To the day of his death Papa teased Mama by saying she imagined the whole thing, for there wasn't a piece of glass out of place by a fraction of an inch. True, the centerpiece was slightly out of line, but Mama could have done that when she dusted.

Papa sold the goats anyway—that very afternoon. They went off in a wagon, unwept, unsung, looking arrogant and self-centered, as if the whole idea had been their own and they were glad to shake the dust of this plebeian spot from their hooves.

Anyway, we didn't need goats to pull a wagon about for us. We had horses.

I literally grew up on the back of a horse. I do not remember when I learned to ride. Probably soon after I could sit alone! We would never have downgraded a horse by considering him a pet, however. He was a friend, a companion, and playmate. To him we would, and did, entrust our lives, our fortunes, and our sacred honor.

Not just every horse, of course. On the farm the law of the sea prevailed in that one horse was reserved for women and children first. At our place, we had several down the years, but the most satisfactory one, the one most nearly human, was Nell.

The stories about her are, literally, legion. We each have our favorites. Sister's has to do with the time she fell off while taking a turn too fast. She maintains that Nell stood over her, nuzzling her like a dog, with great tears in her eyes. Brother's story (related in the presence of a cousin who could have disputed it, had it not been gospel) concerns the way he used to ride Nell bareback, for the cows, and leave to her the whole business of cutting the milk cows out of the herd grazing in the pasture. Not once, according to him, did she make a mistake.

She was a part of all our games, but nowhere so indispensable as when we played on the bag swing. It hung from a tall tree in the yard and, if it was to be any fun, had to be suspended just too high for reaching from the ground. Here Nell came in. We crawled up on her back, and at that height we were just right for the take-off. In order to get to this launching platform, we put a foot on the hock of her hind leg, grabbed her tail, and scrambled up like monkeys. Once aloft, we swung out and away, until it was the next child's turn.

In spite of the hard times we gave her, Nell lived to a ripe age, the last years spent in well-earned retirement; and, at her death, she was accorded an adequate, if not a hero's, funeral.

Of course, if you are talking about pets per se, the best of the lot, the most dearly beloved, the never-tired-of, the easy winner would be dogs.

And Shep was the king of them all, the Number One Dog.

I was the oldest, but even I do not remember when Shep came to us. He was always a part of things, just as Mama and Papa and the house we lived in, and the swing in the box elder north of the house. A large shepherd dog, richly brown, he was noble, regal, large-souled and altogether without fault. We learned to walk clutching his long hair. He would lie and watch our play, his eyes shining with watchful, benign approval. Something of amused tolerance was there, and an alertness to see that our antics brought us to no harm. Mama would be busy in the house and Papa either in town at the Store or in the fields, but Shep was there with us, a background of security and devotion of which we were quite aware. If he left us, which was seldom, one of us would look up to ask uneasily, "Where's Shep?"

Not until he rejoined us could we go back to our play.

He understood every word we said, either to him or to each other. And he sensed our moods as a barometer measures the weather. Only once do I recall his rebelling and that was when I had the idea of hitching him to the little farm wagon, the one originally intended for the goats. He simply sat down on his haunches and looked at me.

"You might as well forget the whole matter," he seemed to say. "I have no intention of doing a thing so completely beneath my dignity."

Finally I gave up, loving him none the less for the stand he took.

Once I said to Papa, "I hope I'm too old to care when Shep dies."

And Papa said gently, "We never get too old to care when something we love leaves us."

As, indeed, we didn't.

Came the time when Shep was an old dog—very, very old. He had rheumatism, and his teeth and sight and hearing were almost gone. He could no longer chase rabbits nor speak firmly to the squirrels who scolded him (if he even heard them) nor tell the jays they were thieving rascals. His pain was our own, as were his deprivations, while we watched him, and Papa said the thing anyone would have said under such circumstances.

"Perhaps we had better put him away."

We were sitting in the kitchen at the time, I recall; the first chill rain of autumn was slithering against the windows. Mama had popped corn and Papa was peeling Winesap apples, cutting off bits and feeding each of us as a parent bird feeds his fledglings. Winter was ahead, and its rigors could promise nothing for Shep, lying now on a blanket close to the kitchen stove.

"It's the kind thing to do," Mama agreed. But I noticed she did not look at Shep as she spoke.

Shep lifted his head. Then with great and unhurried dignity he made his way to Papa and laid his head upon his knee. The eyes which we thought blind looked searchingly into Papa's face. In them was no fear, only understanding compassion. And, clearly as if the words had been spoken, the message went through the room.

"Do not do this thing," the old dog said. "It is against nature."

Even I knew, though dimly, that it was not for himself he interceded, but rather for us: that we should understand the true nature of life so later on—oh, much, much later on—when the experience came to us, we would know, in so far as it is possible for anyone to know, it is not a bad thing to be old if one accepts it as a part of life.

I do not mind being old, he tried to tell us. I do not mind

overmuch, that is. I regret I cannot guard the children as I once did, but I comfort myself with the thought that while the trust was mine, I did it well. Besides, they are now old enough to look after themselves and assume responsibility.

Don't try to tell me the old dog did not speak to us, saying that life was many things—a time for youth and irresponsibility, a time for maturity and responsibility, and a time for old age and resting on one's laurels, and at the last, a quietness, a pause before taking off for the great adventure. Only those who feel they have failed in the earlier stages of life try to keep up the feverish pace of adolescence. Successful old age ends finally, in its own time and in its own way.

We children understood, if not the actual content of his message, the import of it. As a single unit we threw ourselves upon Papa. "Don't," we squawled. "Don't, Papa—please don't—"

Shep, knowing the threat was past, went back to his pallet. Early that winter he went to sleep, very quietly, a good dog and full of years, mourned not only by our family but by our friends and kin as well.

And leaving with us the knowledge that there is a richness of the spirit which comes from nourishing the aged.

All the time Shep ruled our place, we had other dogs, lesser in stature, but good playfellows anyway. They strayed on to our farm, or people gave them to us. I shall never forget the incredulousness which came to me when I learned that people actually bought and sold dogs. It was second only to the shock I experienced when a Big Girl at school gave me some salient facts about the oldest profession.

"Fleas" wandered up to us one day, dirty and hungry and still young enough to be wobbly. He knew us at once for friends and stuck out a little pink tongue hopefully.

"Oh, Papa," we begged. "May we keep him? He looks like such a nice pup."

"That?" Papa asked doubtfully. "You don't want to keep that bag of bones, do you?"

We were very sure we did, arguing the point so convincingly

that he finally gave in. From the depths of our grateful hearts we accorded Papa the greatest honor which was ours to bestow.

"You may name him," we offered graciously.

Papa looked at the small bedraggled pup, covered with burs and caked with mud.

"Why don't you call him Fleas?" he suggested. "He's probably covered with them."

"Fleas" he accordingly became, although I don't recall that he harbored more than the usual number. Naturally, we never thought of rabies shots, license, or registering him. We would have considered any of these as ridiculous pretensions, if not downright questioning of Fleas' dog-honor.

It wasn't long until we knew we had chosen wisely. A few days of good food and unlimited attention and he filled out to a pleasant state of roundness. Never, before or after, did we have such a joyous partner for our games. He entered into our activities with unfailing exuberance, his whole little body quivering with joy merely at being noticed. He even seemed to enjoy being dressed in some of our old baby dresses Mama wasn't sentimental about and donated for that very purpose. That is where we all came near to meeting our downfall.

One morning we buttoned Fleas into a little checked apron. The costume was a natural for the dog—his front legs came through the sleeves, the belt fastened snugly on top. Over the hem his small black tail wagged madly. To complete the ensemble, we put one of Sister's sunbonnets on his head, the strings tied in a firm knot under his chin. Thus accoutered, he was just too utterly fetching, and we sat down to roar with approving laughter at the sight.

The laughter was short-lived. We heard a sharp clip-clop, a sound heralding the coming of Mr. Nicewander, a reactionary if ever one lived, and downright surly besides. Long after most people who could afford to do so were driving automobiles, he stuck to his team of grays and a carriage. Trot, trot. The grays were in line with the front yard fence. We children sat watching him, not venturing a friendly wave as we would have done to any other neighbor. Fleas, reared back on his haunches, watched too. Suddenly the little dog, still clad in bonnet and apron, made a dash for the fence. Over he went like a streak. Straight at the heels of the grays he charged. The one on the near side reared. Mr. Nicewander learned forward, pulling strongly on the reins. No use. Before our horrified eyes the grays lunged forward, mouths wide open, and went careening down the road, with Mr. Nicewander standing up in the carriage, sawing at the reins.

At the horses' heels ran Fleas, yipping wildly, short legs flashing madly under his apron, while his bonnet, which had slipped around until the bow was on top of his neck, dangled under his chin. The team and carriage, with Fleas after it, dipped out of sight behind the lane of walnut trees bordering the road leading up the hill to the house. Mr. Nicewander's pungent expletives, directed alternately at grays and dog, came back to us. Then we could tell he had slowed the team down.

We looked at each other. The crisis was not yet over. The man was not incapable of turning around, driving back to the house, and giving us a good going over. In our fright, I think we even considered the possibility of his using the buggy whip on us. Then we heard something which took our minds off ourselves.

Above the confusion rose the agonized yelping of Fleas. To us this meant only one thing. Mr. Nicewander had beaten the little dog to ribbons, and he was now making his way home, no doubt to die. We shot out into the road to meet our darling, planning to carry him back in tender arms and make his last hours ones surrounded by love and care. Sure enough we could see him coming toward us in a limited, agonized motion which was more rolling than running, his howls of frustration and fear filling the air.

We doubled our speed and finally came to him. I, as befitted the eldest, reached down to scoop him up in my arms, and in so doing discovered the reason for his distress. Not a wound inflicted by Mr. Nicewander at all. Rather, he had become entangled in his bonnet strings in such a fashion as to render one front leg practically useless. All he needed was to have the string untied in order to make him as good as ever. Naturally, the bonnet and apron were beyond repair.

It would be good to report that the experience broke us of dressing up dogs—and cats and chickens as well—in doll or baby clothes. Or, even, that Fleas refused to be a party to such goings-on. Nothing of the sort happened. About the only result was that Mr. Nicewander met Papa in town and told him his crazy kids had made his team run off. No mention of the dog at all. He was in such a temper Papa understood only half he said, but did promise to speak to us about the matter.

We seemed to attract dogs, as honey-bearing flowers draw the bees. There was Dandy, who was left in town by some tourists.

"You kids want him?" a neighbor asked. "He followed me home, and I can't shake him. You can have him if you want him."

There was an unwritten law that we could have three dogs, one for each of us. At that time our census count stood at two, so we accepted the gracious gift without asking permission. Most of our dogs had been just plain dogs, but I know now that Dandy was Pekingese, and probably pedigreed as well. When we got him, he was regal and arrogant, but once he settled on the farm, he lost his princely air. He chased the hens; he gave John and Julius nervous prostration; he wriggled under the summer kitchen and came out all dirt and scratches; he whizzed down to the barn lot, only to be sent packing by a mean-tempered cow; he tripped the hired man (who was carrying two full buckets of milk) and was reprimanded by such a stream of language that he came near leaving us without help; he gave the hummingbirds, coming for the nectar in the petunias, as was their right, a hard time; he sent the squirrels into barking rages. And when there was nothing else to do, he spent the time running in circles, chasing his tail.

Curving over his back in a perfect arc that tail was his pride. He wore it with the conscious air that a man-about-town carried his cane. It was his tail, alas, and his curiosity, which were his undoing.

The day Papa had the hired man get the mower out to cut the alfalfa, he said, "You kids keep that dog inside. He could get hurt, fooling around the mower."

We promised, but our combined vigilance was not enough. We might have known that Dandy would be off to investigate this fresh wonder which clicked so enticingly, and that we could not outwit him. He escaped us and ran headlong to the field.

Perhaps fifteen minutes later a small orange streak came flying across the yard. Dandy passed us with never a look, but we were accustomed to neglect on his part. Straight for the summer kitchen he made, and as he went under, we cried together,

"Look—his tail's gone!"

And so it was.

The hired man reported the details when he came in. The dog had made straight for the sickle, which was high enough to run under. His tail, however, stuck up just far enough to be caught and sliced off.

Three days Dandy stayed under the summer kitchen, ignoring our pleas that he come out. We set water and food out for him, but he ate and drank sparingly. At the end of the third day he emerged, and we raced to meet him. When we saw him—how we laughed. Only a stump of a tail remained, but what was there curled tightly once more over his little orange back.

Laughter broke his spirit, as it has undone many a worthier character. No more chasing anything. After that, he became docile and amenable to discipline. And not half as much fun.

There were so many of those dogs we had when we were children. Each one dear, each one different. There was Hershey, who hopped on the running board of the automobile in town one evening (automobiles had running boards then), and we got him halfway home before Papa knew of his presence. When he did, he laid the law down. We could keep that dog only if it were a *he*. "He-or-she" we kept saying all the way home, hoping for the best. By the time the car stopped, I had named him, in a burst of cleverness I was later to regret, Hershey, which was he-or-she said very fast.

As it happened, he turned out to be a she and before long had some ten or twelve pups, I don't remember which. All I know is, I had never seen so many wriggling bits of puppydom before in all my life. Hershey, grateful to me, no doubt, for having bestowed upon her the dignity of a name, adopted me for her own and followed me if I so much as took a step. The pups, as soon as they found their legs, came after. I was the Pied Piper of the animal world, all right. But Brother adored the great black and white dog, and soon Hershey, the fickle thing, turned to him. Try as I will, I can't remember what disposition we made of the pups.

Then, there was Snookums, a small black and white terrier type who ruled the household like an arrogant old lady in a summer resort. She divided her time equally between field and house—outside mornings, inside afternoon and evenings. She had her favorite chair and nobody would be crude enough to take it; she had her favorite place in the car and sat there, in spite of Mama's complaints about the hair all over everything. She rode horseback with Brother, sitting in front cradled in his arms or behind him, perfectly balanced. She rode by herself, either with or without a saddle.

At the age when all we thought ailed her was middle-age spread, she produced six pups. I regret to say that after the first few days, she turned against them, unable, apparently, to brook rivals even if they were her own flesh and blood. The pups went to good homes and she stayed on, achieving a great age, riding out the changes that came to the family. She was one of the three dogs who raced to meet the grown-up children, coming home for vacations. She was on hand to welcome the first grand-children who held out reaching arms to cry, "Dar Snookie."

"Somebody get those dogs out of the way," Mama would say. "They are the worst nuisances."

She didn't really mean it. She knew that without them, home-coming would lack something—an unchanging quality we wanted to find there; Mama and Papa and the three dogs, the way things had always been. Time and time again we remembered them that way, and the years and the miles that had separated us slipped away. Once more we were children; once more we were at home.

Not long ago I said to Sister, "I dreamed of going home last night. We drove up to the side gate and things were just the same. Mama and Papa came out the door and walked to meet me."

"Were the dogs with them?" Sister asked.

"No," I admitted. "Or, at least, I didn't see them."

"It was a dream all right," she said.

And so it was.

Summer

V.

The Ice Cream Supper

THE seasons were our benevolent despots, governing our actions with fairness and impartial justice, dictating our way of life, assigning us both our duties and our rewards. We pretty well geared our activities to match the pace of their unvarying march.

Promise of spring naturally gave way to fulfillment of summer. The fences around the yard and garden were a solid mass of red or pink or white (or all three) rambler roses, blooming now that June was here. The first vegetables, not counting the lettuce, radishes and young onions, were plumping up, new potatoes were well past the marble stage, early apples were begging to be put into pies and sauce, cherries were hanging among the green leaves, prey to robins and jays, so that we must exercise great diligence and some cunning in order to get our share.

Nobody, at least nobody of our acquaintance, had ever heard of fruits or vegetables out of season. Or flowers either, unless they were ordered from out of town for a funeral. You harvested at the time things were in their prime, working with a frenzied zeal, and, as a matter of course, reaped your benefits at leisure. The fable of the ant and the grasshopper was gospel truth to us, not academic moralizing. If you didn't get the cherries before the birds took over, you jolly well deserved to do without, come winter.

We looked after matters of more general interest with no less prudence and a careful eye on the season as well. Such was the Ice Cream Supper, given by the church.

The best time was June, because, barring some freak of nature, strawberries would then be in their prime. Once or twice the Ladies Aid (who sponsored the event) tried raspberries, but that didn't work out nearly so well. Raspberries tasted all right, but strawberries and ice cream were made for each other, like a couple whose marriage had been prearranged in heaven. A church debt and an ice cream supper were made for each other, too, and nobody disputed the point.

The ladies might decide at their May meeting that the church carpet was badly worn, or we should give more to the missionary we were helping support, or the parsonage needed a new roof. The list was endless for, like the poor, needs were always with us.

Looking back on it now, I think the women wanted a community party and, being eminently practical, saw the Ice Cream Supper as both an excuse and a reward. So they told the preacher and the Sunday school superintendent, and the men of the church talked it over, although this was merely a gesture, for the matter was as good as decided once the women made up their minds. Everyone said it was an excellent idea; the berries should be just right at such and such a time (Saturday night, of course), and the date was accordingly set, like a movable feast on the church calendar.

Naturally the only perfect place for the affair was in the park. And, equally of course, the town band played. It was only looking for an excuse.

The stand from which the serving was done consisted of a large hollow square made of planks, surrounded by other planks which formed the seats for the customers. A few tables were scattered about, set aside for the older people or for those unable, or unwilling, to negotiate the slightly difficult business of getting into the plank seats. There were also chairs and benches for those who wished to sit down, although anyone below the age of twenty-five would have scorned a chair unless he was ill or completely out of things. Of course, the place was lighted with Japanese lanterns, without which, I am convinced, the whole affair would have seemed slightly less than legal.

Among themselves the women worked things out—who was to bring what, and how much. Early in the history of the project, it was decided that vanilla was the only kind of ice cream to consider. Once you started experimenting, the unusual flavors were sure to run out early in the evening, leaving a bunch of disgruntled customers. Besides, vanilla went better with strawberries. Everyone making cakes, however, was dedicated to the doctrine of free enterprise and individual difference. I have only to shut my eyes to see the lot of them—the white cocoanut with the lemon custard filling; the chocolate, so moist and delicious every woman would have given her best piece of cut glass just to get her hands on the secret recipe; the applesauce with black walnuts and cherry preserves; the sponge cakes; the angel foods. Go through the cookbook and you'll find the inventory, those special cakes with fancy icings. But this would not exhaust the list, for some women made them from family recipes, handed down for generations like antique silver.

Every woman who brought a cake was on her mettle, knowing this was the most severe test of the year. Some were known to have made at least three cakes, refusing to ice any of them, and then whip up a fourth before they achieved the standard they had set for themselves. The icing was in itself a special hurdle. For that reason, some women were willing to stick to angel foods which, at least, did not require icing. Others contended this was a cowardly evasion and spoke disparagingly of the ones who tried it.

Even when the cake was finished and iced perfectly, the cook was not out of the woods. There was the delicate business of transporting the masterpiece to its destination with not a bit of icing disturbed. And always there was the danger that a frosting which was perfect when it was put on the cake might, by eating time, have dried out or started to slide tiredly off the cake, or, worst of all, stuck to the container one carried it in. The woman guilty of such a failure never really recovered from the traumatic experience until next year came around, bringing with it a chance for her to redeem herself.

Those who contributed the ice cream had an easier time of it. There was, as everyone knew, only one proper way and that was to make a boiled custard out of whole milk and eggs and vanilla. To this you added cream and then froze. The amounts of ingredients might differ with each woman, but the basic recipe remained pretty much the same. There were hazards, like finding the cream had soured, or allowing the custard to scorch, or getting salt into the mixture at some crucial moment when it was necessary to remove the lid during the freezing period. But, for the most part, ice cream was considered pretty close to foolproof. Although nobody ever came right out and said so, it was assigned to women who weren't the ace cooks in the community.

At last the great night came, and all the cakes and freezers of cream were sitting inside the stand and the women had been assigned to their places of work. About the division of labor there was a pecking order, all the more rigid because it was never put into words. Lowest on the scale were the dishwashers. Later, paper plates were used and considered a great improvement, completely justifying the additional cost. "Really more economical, don't you know, if you count soap and broken dishes and so on." Actually, the innovation came about because the age of rebellion had arrived and the women on dishwashing detail simply refused the job. There were some die-hards, however, who never became accustomed to the use of paper plates. They said the plates gave the ice cream a "taste."

Highest on the totem pole was the cashier, sure to be the smartest woman in the church. And, naturally, the one most trusted, if not always the most beloved. She sat at a small table, with the money in a cigar box, making change and filing away bills which the waitresses brought her. Between her exalted position and the lesser ones who washed the dishes were those who cut the cakes, ran various errands, and waited on the customers. This latter group usually was composed of young matrons who had the energy of the young but not the need to be cruising around the park with their beaux.

The women who cut cakes might not have quite the status of the cashier, but they were tyrants after their fashion, especially where their own contributions were concerned. It was considered quite the thing to ask for a special cake. "I'd like a piece of Mrs. Acton's angel food, please," or "A little of Mrs. Ogden's spice cake." Usually the two ladies were at the cutting table, overhearing the request and acting upon it—if they so wished. Not that they would be crude enough to refuse outright. They just pretended not to hear, or, if that was impossible, they cut off a piece of a similar cake and passed it on to the customer. In substitution, however, they ran a calculated risk. Some sharp-tongued woman thus treated might remark, "I can't see what's all the fuss about Myra Mitchell's cake. Tasted downright ordinary to me."

I found out the hard way about this strategy.

I had come to the Ice Cream Supper filled with conscious virtue. At home, Mama had been so busy with her cake she didn't have time to fix any sort of meal, so she turned things over to me.

"Just put something on the table," she told me. "We'll be eating so much at the supper we don't need much here."

I brought out an assortment of food from ice box and cabinet and afterwards cleaned up. Papa, wishing to recognize my good services, gave me two quarters, entrusting to me the responsibility of buying for Sister and myself.

"What kind of cake do you want, honey?" Mrs. Markham asked when we sat down for our ice cream and cake.

The possession of such a substantial sum of money must have gone to my head.

"I'll have a piece of Mrs. Winter's spice cake," I said, knowing full well I had set my sights on the top of the lot. Mama herself had said that cake was beyond compare.

I oozed gracious condescension as I made my request. Mrs. Winters was going to be greatly pleased to know I chose her above all others, even Mama.

Mrs. Markham looked at me doubtfully, started to speak, and then, apparently, thought better. Instead, she moved toward the lady I had so favored. "She wants a piece of your cake," she said, jerking her head in my direction.

"I'll see if I have any left," Mrs. Winters said, never batting an eye.

Any of it left, indeed! She had just set the cake down. I saw her when she did it, taking the wrappings off as one would un-swath a young princeling for viewing by favored, and royal, subjects. There wasn't even one slice out of it as yet. She wasn't going to fool me with that if-there's-any-of-it-left routine. She fooled me, all right, and in a way I should have known about ahead of time. Without hesitation she turned toward a cake sitting beside hers and cut off a generous slice, handing it to Mrs. Markham.

I ate what was set before me, having had that virtue dinned into me at home. I am sure the substitute was delicious, but for me it had no flavor. I had been fooled, outsmarted, belittled, set aside as naught. At that time I vowed I would never forgive Mrs. Winters. Originally, I even included Mrs. Markham in my displeasure, thinking she might have protested. But common sense prevailed. After all, it was Mrs. Winters' cake, and she had the right to dispose of it as she saw fit.

Later, I would even concede another point. I came to see that her cake had to be saved for the preacher and the doctor and the banker and maybe a politician from the county seat who might decide this was a good place to show his smiling demo-cratic face. To say nothing of other women who would eat, tasting lingeringly, trying (in vain) to unravel the secret of its elusive flavor. She didn't mean to hurt me. She thought I was just a child who wouldn't know the difference, anyway.

Not until after the good lady's death did I get my revenge, and long before that the incident had ceased to matter. I discovered I could add a soupçon of instant coffee to a ready-mix and achieve practically the same results.

If women were unable to figure out the secret of certain desirable flavors, they were quick to pick up the sources of the unpleasant ones. Too much baking powder came in this category. Some frugal souls tried to cover up stinting on egg whites with a liberal slug of baking powder. They always got caught by the bitter flavor which resulted. But this was a minor indiscretion, compared to the other, graver sin.

"I know she used lard instead of butter," the dark whisper went the rounds. "I could taste it. You just can't fool me."

"She said if you used butter to grease the paper you lined your pan with, you can't tell the difference. But anybody can tell, easy as not, the first bite you take."

That was the ultimate awful, the substitution of lard for butter. Some dared the scorn of their fellows, thinking that by using extra vanilla they could cover up the subterfuge. But nobody ever fooled the experts there, either. It was better to stick to butter and use your substitutions in other fields.

The dipping of the ice cream was entrusted to the men, since it was generally considered work too hard for the women. I suspect the men used this as an excuse to be around the excitement and to receive special dispensation in the form of large servings and any number of pieces of cake. They used Mr. Dillion's ice cream dippers, loaned for the purpose. Everyone said wasn't it kind of him, in the next breath downgrading the kindness by saying he wouldn't have had any use for them anyway, for who would have gone to The Dillion Drugs for ice cream when a supper was going on in the park. Which, in the main, was true. Mr. Dillion, recognizing this fact, not only loaned his dippers but usually closed up shop as well.

Occasionally there was someone who didn't fall in line. One woman (the church ladies never found it in their hearts to forgive her completely) actually planned a big dinner for the evening of the ice cream supper, and neither explained nor apologized for her action. If she had even given some logical reason—perhaps out-of-town company she had invited months ago—we would all have felt better. But fortunately such dissenters were few.

Those who came got their money's worth. They ate epicurean food, they visited with friends, they listened to the band. Undoubtedly, the band added to the size of the crowd, but even so, I seriously wonder if the ladies, in the long run, made anything by having them. At the beginning of the concert, they played "The Star Spangled Banner," while they, and we, stood very straight. I can still see the stripes running down the sides of their pants legs, the caps sitting straight on their heads, and the way the cheeks of the boy playing the bass horn puffed out. I used to watch, fascinated, hoping they wouldn't burst. (I *think* I hoped they wouldn't, but I can't be quite sure. Those cheeks were so round, so red, so smooth. Exactly like twin balloons.)

No sooner was this finished than, naturally, the members of the band required nourishment, so they filed down to be refreshed, at the ladies' expense, with ice cream and cake. This happened after every few numbers. By the time they struck up "Home Sweet Home," the signal for the closing of the supper, they must have consumed a sizable amount. But I never heard anyone complain.

Occasionally we had a program. Once a young boy cousin, holding a toy drum, got up and sang a song about a little boy who had bought himself a big bass drum.

"Who knows," sang the lad, "when a war will come? So I want to be ready to play on the drum."

The question was purely academic. We had gone through A War to End All Wars and Make the World Safe for Democracy. Of course another one wouldn't come.

A war did come, and he took part in it. But not by playing the drum.

Although it was, of course, not always possible to arrange things so well, anyone with a grain of sense knew the best time for the Ice Cream Supper was when the moon was full. Not only were fewer Japanese lanterns required at such times, but the occasion was better adapted for what the young people considered the prime purpose of the affair.

That was the pairing off of couples.

The supper served, in fact, as a sort of coming-out ball, a presenting of eligible maidens to Society. Here the boys had an opportunity to see that girls who, only last year, had been playing with other girls had grown anywhere from two to four inches, were wearing their hair in the latest style, and had persuaded their mamas to let out their dresses. Or, what was even more important, had a new dress for the occasion.

Sophisticated societies call this a debut; primitive people frankly label it as puberty rites; we simply took note of who was eyeing whom, knowing that, given a year or two, he would be buying her ice cream. And those who had eyed last year, or the year before, now marched up with money in hand, ready to treat the girl of his choice.

As in the case of all such matters, the stages were well defined. The girls, at their first go-round, stayed in groups. The boys came to them. Every girl knew her cue was to pretend to ignore them, giggling incessantly, tossing her curls over her shoulder. Which of course, fooled the boys not at all. The time had not yet come for treating by the boys. This was a matter of pure economics. They ate separately, tossing comments back and forth. Once this was over, they again gathered in groups. The few daring ones who did pair off risked catcalls and laughter from the boys without either the courage or the cash to enable them to treat a girl themselves.

For the older ones, there was also a well-defined pattern. A boy would sidle up to a girl, clear his throat, and ask if he might buy her some ice cream. Together they made their way to the stand, conscious of the awareness all the mamas had of their action. It was as good as a declaration of intentions. The girl's mama, and the boy's as well, tried to take the whole matter lightly. But occasionally this was difficult, especially if the son— or daughter—was accompanied either by a Real Catch or, the reverse situation, a matter to be greatly regretted, by someone less than worthy.

For the younger ones, the approach was less ritualistic. We played games—drop the handkerchief, hide-and-seek (although that was really for the very young), and a more or less sadistic one called Flying Dutchman. For this we stood in a circle, hands linked. A couple, also with linked hands, made the round of the circle and finally, when the spirit moved them, struck a pair of linked hands. The couple so chosen must start in the opposite direction, flying around the circle. The trick was to beat the other couple back to the starting point, holding to each other's hands, of course. Failure to beat meant you were "It."

Once my partner and I ran with more speed than judgment, colliding with another couple so violently that the girl's glasses sailed off into the darkness. We all had to stop and help hunt them, an activity which the owner could not join, for without her glasses she couldn't see her hand before her face. Finally someone located them under a bridal wreath bush, miraculously unbroken. By this time our elders were alerted and decreed we should play this game no more.

Toward the time for the supper to end, we began to edge up closer to the stand. We knew that before long our mamas would call us over to help clean up what was left. No need to drag stuff home, they wisely decided. Besides, any woman who carried so much as a crumb of her cake back with her would have lost caste forever, not only with her friends but in her own eyes as well.

Finally it was all over. Substantial plates were sent to the ill, the shut-in, the aged. Dippers clanked sharply against empty ice cream freezers. Men carried the salt-and-ice mix away to empty in the road so as not to hurt the grass. Women were busy setting things to rights. The cashier reported the take to the waiting women, and everyone chortled with delight. Families loaded up their children and the empty freezers and cake containers, and everyone took off.

Of course, the ride home was a good time for talking things over.

"We did real well," Mama told Papa. She named a sum.

"I should say so. Have any special place to put it?"

"A carpet for the church aisle, I think. Although that means trouble. Mrs. Metzger wants solid red and Mrs. Poole is all for beige with a green design."

"Well," Papa said, "knowing Mrs. Metzger, I'd say the red was good as down."

"I wouldn't be so sure," Mama told him. "I expect the fur will fly before the thing is settled."

That was her way of describing a battle. "The fur flew," she would report and we all knew there had been a Real Row.

She sighed a little now, but more in resignation than in despair. Church feuds were a part of the whole business; you took the bitter with the sweet. Not only that, but for some, I suspect, they were the spice of life.

"I never in all my life saw anything like the way Lin ate," Mama went on, shifting to another subject. (Lin was the current hired man.) "I do believe he came back half a dozen times."

"That much more money in the treasury," Papa reminded her.

"We'll probably have to call Dr. Carney in the night," Mama said. "I just hope he doesn't charge it to the church."

I think perhaps we children went to sleep on the way home, the combination of exercise, excitement, and gorging having taken its toll. Finally we were home and shaken awake and made to go inside, even though, at the moment, we would gladly have slept the night where we were. But go inside we did and wash our feet (we had, of course, taken our baths before going to the Supper, but our feet would most certainly have got dusty in the park) for tomorrow was Sunday and we must be up early and ready for Sunday school on time.

And so, it was over for another year.

There must have been variations on the general theme—years when it rained, or the strawberries were below standard, or I was sick and unable to go. But looking back, I was always there, and things went well, and the routine was unvaried. I couldn't begin to know how old I was at any specific one; time seems to have held a fused quality, one supper melting into another so smoothly that I was, perhaps, always ten years old. Yes, ten would have been an ideal age for attending an ice cream supper in a Missouri small-town park. You would be large enough to be turned loose, more or less, and not yet old enough to worry about whether you would have a new dress or a date.

Maybe that's the way with most childhood memories. You are forever the same age, or no age at all and, at the same time, all the ages you ever lived. Not only you, but your family and friends and kin as well, imbedded in an ageless immortality that will remain always the same, like wax flowers under a glass dome; like the picture hanging over the bed in Mama and Papa's room. Two little girls, painted in delicate pastels, clinging to each other, fixed in a pattern of fright and mutual concern as they regarded a huge butterfly just above their heads.

Years later I saw the original picture, a black and white steel engraving, and realized the print I had known in my childhood was only a detail of it. Actually, the little girls were alone in a forest, and the reason for their fright was a herd of deer. But no matter what the original picture was, reality, for me, will always remain two small girls, drawing back in innocent terror at the sight of a butterfly.

VI.

And on the Seventh Day—

IF we skipped our baths on the Saturday night of the Ice
Cream Supper, it was a special dispensation because, ordinarily, Mama took us in hand then no matter how much she
was given to letting us slide along under our own power during
the week. Come Saturday, there was a great gouging of ears,
wails of "Ouch, Mama, you're killing me," and a tremendous
air of purpose in the bathroom. You got clean, or else.

Actually, Sunday started on Saturday. There were bread and
cakes to bake, chickens to dress, churning to do. Round and
round and round you turned the handle of the churn until, just
when you thought the cause was hopeless, there was a watery
sound inside the churn which told you the butter had separated,
leaving the buttermilk and the golden globules of butter apart
from each other. At that stage, Mama entered the picture. It
would have been a form of blasphemy for a hired girl or a
child to take up the butter or to work it. This latter operation
was carried out with the aid of cool, clear water and a wide
wooden paddle Papa had carved for Mama immediately after
their marriage and which, down the years, was a kitchen tool
for which Mama had the greatest sentiment. Once the milk was
worked out of the butter, salt was added in judicious amounts,
for too much indicated a careless cook. Butter coloring, too, was
frowned upon, as it was a sure sign you hadn't taken proper
care of your cream. Finally the butter was ready to be molded.

Some used wooden molds for this purpose, with imprints of flowers or other decorations. Mama was more original. She shaped the pat into a rectangular blob of yellow, rounded it off at the corners and sides, and then, quick as anything, put her own design on the surface. This she did by making a dent with the paddle on sides and top and then turning the pat to make a second one. (I tried it once with oleo, and what a funny, wavering mess I made.) When it was finished, the mound of butter, approximately a pound in weight, bore the curved prints, shaped like giant parentheses, set close together. The sides glistened with moisture, and the taste was utterly delectable.

We also gathered vegetables of the season and hulled or strung or went through whatever preliminaries were necessary to make them ready for cooking. These we stored in the ice box. The house must be cleaned and the beds changed. Our legs ached with running errands, and by bathtime and bedtime we were ready to call it a day.

We counted all effort well spent, for the next day was Sunday, and even waking up had a feeling of excitement, a bustle of purpose. Breakfast and dishes were pushed through with incredible speed, regardless of our tendency to dillydally other days. Then we dressed, wearing our best dresses, which were automatically labeled our Sunday ones. We were aware of them and of the faint, enticing rustle of our starched petticoats against our small bodies. My hair was braided—so tight it was a wonder I could shut my mouth—and then tied with ribbons; Sister's curls were also beribboned. And of course Brother was brushed and slicked up until he fairly shone.

We measured the season by the roadside flowers. In spring, a succession of dandelions, violets, and crab-apple blossoms, pink and white in thickets; summer, ushered in by the wild roses, to be succeeded by daisies, a few thistles, black-eyed Susans, wild iris (which for no good reason we called snake flower); fall, heralded by sunflowers, asters, and goldenrod; and winter, marked by the berries of the bittersweet and a few leaves hanging to the trees, and later either snow or the drabness of grass, waiting out the winter. Sometimes Papa stopped and let us gather flowers, but never on our way to church. That might make us late. Usually they had wilted by the time we got them home, and I was all sneezes and hives. (I never associated this with allergies, of which we had not yet heard.) Still, we persisted.

Anyway, nobody would have wanted to delay our arrival at church. Our best chums would be waiting there, and we would promenade up and down, exchanging news of the week just passed, keeping our eyes on the open door the while. The minute the superintendent took his place in front we scuttled in like so many chickens being shooed into a coop. We knew better than to stay outside after services had begun, just as we knew better than to choose a back seat, a procedure to which Grandpa referred as "Sitting on the coal oil cans." This harked back to the early days when fuel for stoking the church lamp was coal oil, kept in cans in the back of the church. To sit there branded you as unregenerate and, although the term was not yet invented, a juvenile delinquent. The most amazing thing is I cannot, even yet, feel entirely comfortable in the back seat of a church.

So we marched in and took a seat well down toward the front, filled with virtue and anticipation, noting with satisfaction that Mrs. Osgood had not yet arrived.

Mrs. Osgood was a large woman, weighing close to two hundred pounds and looking even larger. She walked with her head held high, her shoulders straight and square, her hips swaying a little. Another woman of her size and build might have shrunk back in corners, trying not to call attention to herself. Mrs. Osgood scorned any such cowardly approach to life.

Not given to promptness in any endeavor, at church she was almost invariably late. Usually the choir had started before she arrived; with what I have since learned to rate as perfect timing, she came to the front door at the exact moment of the opening of the first hymn. Pausing there, she waited until the most stirring portion had been reached and then marched down the aisle, walking lightly on the balls of her feet in spite of her great weight, swaying a little from the hips, her head keeping time with the music as she walked.

At the exact point where the sentiment of the hymn seemed to merit it, she would shout, "Hal-le-*lu*-jah!" Having done this, she would seat herself, pick up a hymn book, and join the other members of the congregation who, until she came, had been bumbling along in decorous unanimity.

I would have crawled under my bench in shame had Mama or any of the kin ventured so much as a meek "Amen" except where custom dictated. But for me, Mrs. Osgood's exhibition lent spice and excitement and a sense of joy to the service. I suspect it was a sentiment shared by my elders even though they sometimes laughed at her and some of the more proper ones had spoken to her about the matter. They might as well have saved themselves the trouble, so finally they gave up. A good thing, too, for although we were professed followers of the Brothers Wesley, I think in matters of music we leaned toward Mr. Billy Sunday.

The magnificent hymns of Charles Wesley might have offered to the struggling workmen of England a brighter approach to religion than did the formal chanting of the Church of England. But that was all a long way off, both in distance and in time, from our church, and we children of a later day and brighter destiny found the old songs a bit dull. Where Mr. Wesley would have set us to inquiring with proper humility and reasonable doubt,

> "Depths of Mercy can there be,
> Mercy, still, reserved for me?"

we preferred to proclaim blithely and with complete confidence that we were "The Child of a King." Doubtless it was to our musical as well as our spiritual discredit that we preferred not only the sentiment of the latter but the tune as well.

Not that we were lost in a maze of sweetness and light, either. We had problems, and we recognized them. Our songs were our refuge, our comfort, our strength in time of trouble. Mr.

Wesley was speaking to miners and laborers. We were farmers and small-town business people. We knew our problems and our needs.

Perhaps one of the greatest disasters that can befall a rural community is a prolonged summer drought. There is something so final, so irrevocable about a crop failure. If a merchant does poorly in July, he always can hope things will pick up in August. But a farmer has to wait a full year before trying again. Not only that, but rural people sometimes felt the drought was a punishment sent upon them by the Lord, for sins they did not even know for sure they had committed. Since Papa had a business in town and farmed as well and since rural economy is closely interrelated, our family suffered doubly the cruel barbs of fate or, if you wish, the displeasure of the Lord. At such times I examined carefully my own list of sins, wondering whether to lay the current lack of rain to my getting more than my share of strawberry shortcake or evading my turn to do the dishes.

One summer stands out from all the rest, with crops withering in hot and merciless sun and ponds drying up. Each night the sun sank in a bright blaze of color, but we took small comfort in its beauty, recalling the jingle, "Red at night, sailor's delight." We were not concerned about the well-being of sailors in our community.

By mid-July a kind of desperate hopelessness had settled over us all. Even if rain came now, which was unlikely at this time, it could not save the corn. The best we could hope for was fresh pasture, which would prevent having to sell off some of the stock at ruinous prices. Everyone said, though, that it wouldn't rain until September, now that it had held off so long. In this mood we settled down to wait.

Some people even stopped coming to church, saying it was just too hot, but the more hardy continued. Among this number, of course, was our family. We went as usual, but we averted our eyes from the ruined fields and talked of other things besides the heat and burnt-up crops.

Then there came a Sunday so hot and breathless that even

we debated staying at home. Finally, we decided to go, however, and at church found people numbed and hopeless. So much so, in fact, that instead of standing for the first song, as was our custom, we sat.

"A wonderful Savior is Jesus my Lord," we intoned with more resignation than confidence in our voices.

> "He hideth my soul in the cleft of the rock
> That shadows a dry thirsty land—"

At that point Mrs. Osgood, with her perfect sense of timing, appeared at the church door. Pausing briefly, she started up the aisle, rocking on her toes, joining in the singing as she came. Just as she reached her pew, she let out a "Hallelujah!" that shook the rafters.

Suddenly we were all on our feet, rocking on our toes a little, singing at the top of our voices.

> "He hideth my soul in the depths of His love,
> And covers me there with His hand."

"Hallelujah," Sister Osgood shouted, and the last one of us, even the proper ones who had tried to stop her upon occasion, did a totally unexpected thing.

"Hallelujah," we shouted, and then went back and sang the song again, dwelling on the part about the "dry thirsty land."

This time we weren't singing with patient endurance but with hope and good cheer.

It rained that night. Not enough to break the drought, but sufficient to help the pasture. I thanked Mrs. Osgood, along with God, for the blessing we received. Scoffers, naturally, will contend that she could have no possible connection with the reversal of the weather pattern. That is entirely beside the point. There is no doubt but that she brought us courage and hope at a time when we were woefully short on those desirable commodities.

We were not always beset with droughts. One summer we went to the opposite end of the ledger to have what those of us who went through it still call, simply, The Wet Year. It rained, and it rained, and it rained, and then it rained some more. The Christian Church, our chief rival in the Lord's Work, set three separate dates for their Sunday school picnic, only to be deluged every time. Papa, who was superintendent of our Sunday school at the time, suggested jokingly that they should throw in with us Methodists, hoping thereby to come off with nothing more than a light sprinkle. Made in fun, his suggestion was taken seriously. Accordingly, we had our picnic together.

The day turned out to be just about the only completely sunny one of the entire summer. Great joy was felt in both camps, as we met to consume untold quantities of fried chicken and baked ham and potato salad and cakes and pies, washed down by goodness knows how many gallons of lemonade. There were, of course, some reservations. The Methodists, I regret to report, took credit for the bright weather, implying the Lord had chosen to smile upon them, while the Christians went about all day with eyes trained on the sky. We children took the whole thing for what it was, a chance to have a good time, and squeezed every moment of happiness from it. The story is told that in the afternoon a short program was held at which time the Christian flock sang "Shall We Gather at the River," while the Methodists responded with "There Shall Be Showers of Blessings." I don't remember this, so I cannot vouch for the selections.

Papa said the Lord was smiling on us because we got together; he said he always did think there should be one church. For once, I didn't agree with him. Church union was a perfectly horrible idea—it would mean just one picnic every summer. As things stood, we always went to our own and usually got invited to the other by friends who were members of the rival church.

For rivals we were. Make no mistake about that. This attitude may not have embodied the essence of the Christlike spirit, but it did keep things from getting dull. The chief quarrel we had with each other was that both accused the other of proselyting. I tried hard to work out a definition of this grave sin in my own heart and mind, without success. Mostly it was a word that wore horns and a tail and exuded the faint odor of brimstone. I was a good-sized girl before it began to dawn on me that what passed for proselyting in a member of the Christian Church was simply "Divine concern for souls" in a Methodist. I was much older before I realized the definition was reversible.

In late summer came the Revival Meeting, lasting a week. (Longer, if some of the unregenerated showed signs of relenting.) In our church we tried to get the Presiding Elder or some other preacher of note to conduct at least a few of the services. (In 1939, when the North and South Methodist Churches decided to forget all about "The Late Unpleasantness" and merge, we changed the title Presiding Elder to District Superintendent. Granted this is more accurate, I still think it less impressive. I always envisioned a Presiding Elder as sitting on one of the top steps nearest the throne; a District Superintendent could be off in a corner with any group of saintly executives.) We also tried to import a singer, although this was desirable rather than absolutely necessary. The choir actually considered this latter practice a reflection on their merits, an attitude often shared by some of the older members. The latter group's reasoning probably came from the fact that the imported singer was usually a very young, good-looking man who distracted the girls to the point where their minds were not on their eternal souls.

Naturally, the Christians also had their revival. Here we observed the most meticulous etiquette. Each church must give the town time to recover from a revival—and, what was more important, to lapse into a state of sin sufficient to justify another one—before having its own hitch at saving souls. It never occurred to us that we might have had a union meeting with profit. Each of us conducted our own safari for souls, unaided—and unhindered—by the rival church. True, we attended the other meeting, as members of the other church attended ours, but we sat with fingers crossed and listened no more than we could help to the terrible threats or siren promises of the rival minister.

Although it was a truly good thing to bring any sinner into the fold, there was a well-recognized scale of values placed upon them, a situation completely understood by the visiting minister, if such we had. Meek, tender young boys and girls of impeccable virtue meant little credit for the preacher in charge. Each revival meeting harvested this crop, already made ready by mamas and Sunday school teachers. A notch above them were the young husbands who, until now, had seen fit to do little more than attend church with their wives. Everyone knew these good women had been working on their husbands and gave the ministers little credit. The real test was the hardened unregenerate, usually a young blade possessing great charm and an unabashed capacity for worldly pleasures. Highest on the scale were the hopeless middle-aged ones long since despaired of by everyone, even the members of their own families. The visiting ministers were aware of these gradations, and if they brought in only run-of-the-mill sinners, the regular minister might just as well have conducted the meeting and saved the church that extra expense.

Perhaps it was the sinners who got the most enjoyment out of these meetings. They could not fail to be aware of their own importance at this time, as sure of their worth as politicians with favors to bestow. Certainly, the rejoicing which came with the entry of a lost sheep into the fold must have been sweet to those who, all the rest of the year, enjoyed little favor. Nobody could blame them for holding out until the last night, thereby insuring for themselves a week of flattering attention. During the revival it was permissible, nay even obligatory, that pretty girls (already members of the church) have dates with boys ordinarily frowned upon. The purpose was to bring them closer to salvation. It was amazing how the girls entered into the spirit of the occasion, bearing their cross meekly.

There were two types of sinners who gave us the most trouble, both fortunately rare. The first was the man—it was nearly always a man—who was a thorn in our righteous sides. Without him in our midst, we might have discussed freely the sins which walked open and unashamed in Kansas City and St. Louis and other large cities, congratulating ourselves that we were not as they were.

With the presence of a bona fide sinner in our midst, such self-congratulation was denied us. It was always worse if such a one looked and felt in top shape and continued to prosper. In Kansas City, let us say, we could have retired to the suburbs and left sin to its own territory; in our town, we couldn't get ourselves far away enough to be out of sight of it.

There was the other extreme, the sinner who was overpenitent. He went forward to the mourners' bench every time there was a meeting, whether in our church, in the Christians', at camp meetings, or the churches of other towns. He confessed regularly and promised to do better and joined the church. He joined rival churches, and then he came back to rededicate himself to the church of his original choice. The preacher had to receive him in good faith—the Bible was very clear on such matters.

But these were exceptions. For the most part we took our revivals seriously. The faithful were gathered in, and a new year started. In a way, it was a little like house cleaning.

Sometimes the visiting ministers achieved results beyond even their own expectations.

For instance, once we had a young man come to us, earnest and determined to make good, one of those hell-fire-and-damnation kind. You could fairly smell the fire and brimstone as he talked, see the smoke curling around the church. Not one of us but could have given a good description of Satan, down to his cloven hoofs and forked tail.

Ordinarily, we would have relaxed comfortably during such sermons, assured in our own minds that they were directed against the really wicked people who didn't come to church and more than likely lived off somewhere else, like Kansas City. This young divine denied us any such smug comfort. It was for us the Everlasting Fire burned, and we were not allowed to forget it.

"We are all sinners," he assured us, looking about the church as if seeking to find some specific target on which to pin his statement. Then, evidently having found one which satisfied him, he pointed his finger at Brother and a young cousin. "Even those two young boys," he told us, "innocent and fair and lovely though they may seem to you, are not safe from the Devil and his wiles."

The two boys so singled out turned pale, squirmed, and sat straighter. Instinctively I looked over my shoulder, half expecting to see His Satanic Majesty lifting a floor board of the church in order to get at his prey. Once outside of the church, however, I could tell myself we were in no great danger. True, I could remember a few specifics—the time I wore my best hair ribbon when I wasn't supposed to, the piece of cake I had snitched—but the list was neither long nor imposing. I felt reasonably safe. I dismissed the threat to Brother and the cousin as ridiculous. Nuisances they might be, and great ones to tattle, but hardened sinners, no.

It so happened that the cousin and his mama and papa came home with us that day for dinner. In the middle of the afternoon we missed the boys, so the parents set off to look for them, the other children tagging along. We were guided by a great thumping sound which led us, eventually, to where the two small boys sat back of the hay barn, each with a hammer, and between them an empty nail keg. All around the ground were nails at intervals of about six inches.

"What on earth are you doing?" Papa asked. Those were new nails, meant for mending the barn roof, and the dampish earth would do them no good.

Brother rose to explain, as befitted the son of the house.

"It's because of the Devil," he explained. "The preacher said he would get us, and we're fixing this place to play in so if he comes for us he'll stick himself and go back."

Even we children knew this was no time for laughter. I, for one, was glad Papa took them off for a private, and kindly I am sure, lecture on theology, geared to their understanding.

The revival finally ended, a satisfying number of converts joined the church, and we pronounced the young minister a success. And then, with him gone, we slipped back comfortably to listen to our own preacher, who knew us so well he didn't have to remind us of our sins.

Another special occasion in our church was Children's Day. Mama took this into account when Miss Mattie came to do the spring sewing.

"Let's see," she said, "I think we'll make your dresses like this." She held up a pattern. "That will be all right to wear anywhere and still be nice enough for Children's Day.'"

Miss Mattie got down on her knees stiffly and began to measure. Sister took to fittings like a duck to water, but I wiggled and stood all uneven and must have made a great deal of trouble for the poor seamstress. But all was forgiven once the dress was finished (white, of course) and I stood up, come Children's Day, to say my piece and join in the singing.

Usually this program was much of a pattern, with those who grew too old to say pieces being replaced by moppets who had just mastered the art, and songs whose words and titles were different but whose sentiment remained the same. One year we did try an innovation which turned out far from well. It was decided that instead of standing either on the platform or to the front rows to sing, we should come up the church aisle, warbling as we made our way. In this endeavor we were doomed from the start. Being so far removed from the piano we were never, even for one moment, on the same beat with the accompanist. There were other, minor difficulties. One of the marchers tripped and ran bawling to her mama; an imp of Satan (male, of course) pinched the warbler just in front of him, thus introducing into the song a mighty "Ouch," certainly never written into the score; in our haste and eagerness, we came up the aisle at a full gallop.

After that the program planners were satisfied to do things in the old familiar way.

Another great occasion was Ladies Aid, which met each month in the homes of members. Only at house-cleaning time were such pains taken as the hostess felt were necessary in preparation for this visitation. There were always some members, their curiosity exceeded only by their cunning, who took advantage of the occasion to give the house a thorough casing.

They got upstairs by pretending they thought you meant them to leave their hats up there when all the time they could see the downstairs bedroom was being used for that purpose; they developed a coughing fit which necessitated a trip to the kitchen for a drink, passing up the cut-glass pitcher of water sitting handily on the sideboard; and of course, they had to go to the bathroom. Such unprincipled women were not above opening closet doors, so it was necessary to be prepared. Knowing this, you cleaned thoroughly and let them wander.

Later the organization's name was changed to the Missionary Society, and the members took to heart the cause of the wide world. It was our version of the Peace Corps, our Marshall Plan, our Dr. Schweitzer, and our Tom Dooley, and the dollars clicked in the collection plate. But make no mistake—the name and aims might have changed but the character remained the same. Missionary Meeting or Ladies Aid, whichever you chose to call it, was still Society. You served your choice food, and everyone wore her Sunday dress, and a good time was had by all.

Nothing was more memorable than Sunday company. This was of two kinds. First, there was the planned-for variety you asked a day or two ahead. For them you cleaned the house, cooked various delectables, and left a roast, or chicken, or both in the oven. Of course, everybody had a baked ham on hand. You stretched the table as far as it would go, used the best table linen, dishes, and silver, brought choice jams and relishes and canned stuff out of the cellar, and then took off to church, trying to act as if you hadn't gone to a bit of trouble. Of course, you fooled no one because every woman asked had herself, upon occasion, whipped through a similar set of preliminaries.

At such times the preacher often came, raising the whole affair to the status of an occasion. Everyone was on his best behavior; because of the number of guests, the children usually ate either at the second table or on the porch or in the kitchen, depending on the season.

The real tour de force, however, consisted in asking company at church. Just like that, on the spur of the moment. Mama would move out of her pew as soon as the benediction was over with a look of purpose in her eye. "Come home to dinner with us," she would say to Mrs. Upjohn or Mrs. Carmody, or Mrs. Barrett, or maybe all three. It sounded very offhand, as if she had thought about it only at the moment, which fooled the women not at all. They knew she had got little out of the sermon, sitting there checking off the size of the roast and the state of the house. Now and then a woman who did this was suspect, the sort of person who wanted to show off how well she kept house and what a good table she set. Mostly you were saved from this accusation, however, by the fact that at such times you asked only your closest friends, and they knew the details of your housekeeping without being told.

Actually, these dinners usually turned out to be the best of all. In an excess of energy, Mama literally loaded the table with all she could lay hands on.

"It's no use," a visiting woman would protest, "you can't get another thing on that table."

Whereupon Mama would rearrange things so that she was able to edge in a dish of peach pickle—"sweet pickle," we called them.

I remember these dinners clearest of all. The relaxed ease of friends breaking bread together; the special atmosphere that goes with unexpected, and pleasant, surprises; the quick flash of talk and the quicker one of laughter; the warmth. Usually the guest list was small enough that we children could eat at the first table, or, if it grew larger, we could serve buffet and give the whole affair the air of a picnic. Afterwards the women helped with the dishes (although Mama protested, halfheartedly, that they need not), and more visiting took place. It was here they came to grips with community news.

"Wonder why Martha Hanks wasn't at church?"

"Oh, didn't you *know?*"

Lifted eyebrows, knowing looks, the coded message that Mrs. Hanks was going to have a baby. And weren't they dumb to think I hadn't caught on?

"Melinda Brooks came home last night, just about dusk, they say. Slipped in the kitchen door, and she'd been crying."

"Well, what do you expect—after all, she married a Brooks."

There was happier talk—of engagements and weddings and babies and new recipes and household hints. And laughter—always, always plenty of that.

Outside if it was summer, and in the front living room around the fireplace if the weather was cold, the men talked politics and crops and prices and items read in the *Star*. By and by it was time for them to leave and we watched them and waved, and the happiness the day had brought both went with them and stayed behind knowing no division or diminishing.

I am willing to admit that the fault lies within me now when I say I do not find in the present-day church service the same sense of adventure I once knew. It's correct and departmentalized and dignified. (We never would have dreamed of departmentalizing Sunday school classes, nor could we have got by with telling people where to go had we tried it. We met upstairs, which we called quite simply "The Church" and was, naturally, one room, or in the basement whose flimsy partitions made no pretense of cutting out sounds. Any teacher worthy of his job had jolly well better talk loud enough to be heard above the other classes.) Today we are organized and carry on like big business.

For church services now there is a printed program which is followed to the letter. Starred spots at intervals indicate the points at which worshipers may be seated. If there isn't a star at the place where you came in, you can just stand there and wait in the vestibule for the cue to follow the usher—complete with discreet smile and white boutonniere—to the seat he says it's right for you to have.

The other morning I arrived at church a little late, to be met by the usher who indicated I should stand quietly until the hymn was finished.

"We're marching to Zion," choir and congregation were affirming.

But their words held no real conviction. The only place they seemed sure of getting was to the end of the song.

Something rose up in me. A great wish, a wild urge, an almost uncontrollable impulse. In spite of the restraining usher, in spite of the complete dearth of stars on the program, it was all I could do to keep myself from pushing open the door and starting up the church aisle, swaying a little as I walked, my head high, my shoulders square, singing as I went:

> "Beautiful, beautiful Zion,
> Hal-le-*lu*-jah—"

I probably would have broken up the service had I been able to push past the usher, which is doubtful. On the other hand, it might not have worked too badly. After the first shocked horror, the choir and congregation might even have joined in with me. And had they done so, they all probably would have sounded a little more confident about really getting to Zion.

VII.

Thicker Than Water

THE one Sunday we missed church as a matter of course was Family Reunion Day. That could fall at any time during the summer, from June to August.

We loved our paternal grandfather and grandmother dearly and went to see them regularly. They, in turn, visited us. But Papa's family was more scattered and less given to reunions. When these did occur, they were smaller in size and certainly more restrained than were the gatherings on Mama's side of the house.

When Mama's family got together, it was no light undertaking. If we included only the immediate family the number would be impressive enough, but if we went farther afield on the genealogical chart, taking in great-aunts and great-uncles, together with their offspring, their kin, their in-laws, and their kin to kin, the gathering could assume tremendous proportions. For instance, one of the great-uncles had married three times, the first wife being Grandpa's sister. We continued to claim kin with him, the two successive wives, their children and their kin. I defy anyone, except perhaps Grandma and Grandpa, to sort out the far-flung relationships represented. Early in my attendance at these gatherings I gave up trying and simply called everyone who looked three years older than I "Cousin" unless, of course, the person so addressed announced that he (or she) bore another relationship. Cousin, however, was always safe, since that was the title we bestowed on kin to kin as well as blood relations.

As a child, I attended these occasions without question. But when I got to the age where I preferred being with friends of my own choosing, I began to think they were getting a bit out of hand. I remember rebelling only once, however, and that must have been when I was just entering my teens. I protested; I think I even said, defiantly, that I wasn't going.

Which was a mistake on my part. We just didn't stand up and say those words to Mama. She had absolutely no fear of injuring our psyche even had she known we had one, which she didn't.

"We'll have no such talk," she said firmly. (Being a parent must have been a richly satisfying experience then.) "The very idea—what would Cousin Hester think if you stayed away when she'd gone to so much trouble and all. You'll have a wonderful time—there'll be more than a hundred there. Just like going to the fair."

There was absolutely no resemblance between the two, and I was not to be soothed by *that* comparison.

"All they'll do is kiss everybody, and talk old times,'" I said. "I don't want to go."

"Want to or not, you're going," Mama told me briskly. "Now what will you wear? Oh, I know—I'll let out the hem of your dotted swiss. You've grown inches this summer."

I was relenting in spite of myself, what with being allowed to wear my best dress and having my added inches recognized.

"All right, I'll go," I said, giving in graciously. "But I tell you one thing—I'm not going to kiss Cousin Marvin."

I don't know why I chose to discriminate against that particular cousin, really just an in-law. He was an inoffensive person, mild and kindly, who had no more wish to kiss me than I had to kiss him.

"Suits me fine," Mama told me casually. "Probably suits him, too."

So I went to the reunion, wearing my best dress, and had a fine time.

We liked the smaller gatherings better, although goodness

knows these were large enough, since Mama had six sisters and two brothers. By the time the aunts and uncles—blood and in-law—and Grandpa and Grandma and the cousins assembled, it was enough to fill anyone's house and yard. Naturally the hostess was not expected to provide single-handed for so inclusive an occasion. Everyone brought a basket, of course, which was wonderful because Mama's sisters were all marvelous cooks. But we paid for this, as one must pay for all life's good things. We had to eat something of everything, so as not to hurt anyone's feelings. If you passed up any dish, even bread and butter sand-wiches, an aunt's reproachful eye was sure to be cast in your direction while she asked, "What's the matter? Don't you *like* my bread?"

"Oh, yes," we would assure her, "we do like it."

Then we would feel honor-bound to take two instead of one sandwich when, actually, we really didn't want a bite of bread. And we'd eat them both because either the aunt or one of her children would be watching us, noticing if we so much as threw a crumb to the birds.

Even now I cannot eat smorgasbord with any peace of mind. It does no good to tell myself that I don't have to taste everything on that table, for all the time I don't really believe it. I half expect a cousin of the cook to be lurking somewhere in the wings, ready to report any item I skip.

There was this about cousins—they did keep up with you. Best you behave at a party or any other public function for there was always a cousin handy to go home and tell on you. Of course, he told his mama, who, naturally, knew it was her duty to tell your mama, so the word finally got back where it could do the most good, losing nothing in the telling.

It was a cousin (at her first party and lurking around the fringes so that I had forgotten about her) who told her mama, who, of course, passed it on to my mama (for my own good, naturally) that I had sat in front of the house in a parked auto-mobile for all of a half-hour. With that Mitchell boy. And everybody knew what he acted like around girls.

Except, he hadn't acted Like That around me at all. There

were two courses open to me. I could believe his reputation in such matters was totally unjustified, a story hatched up by old biddies with nothing better to do, or I could admit I simply wasn't the kind to inspire him to Act Like That. It did not occur to me then that his reputation might just be the result of wishful thinking on the part of other girls whose experience with him had duplicated my own. For goodness sakes, he hadn't even tried to hold my hand!

I had not decided which course of action to take when Mama got me aside to give me a Good Talking To. I listened with downcast eyes as Mama gave me information she doubtless considered quite frank and free and calculated to arm me for what lay ahead. Actually it was vague and general, completely lacking in the folk wisdom exchanged by the girls at school. I think all the time she suspected my experience with the Mitchell boy had been downright flat instead of wildly exciting.

Not only were cousins omnipresent in social functions—they were right on the job at school. The P.T.A., now regarded as a must for parents who would know how their offspring fare, was entirely unnecessary in our day. A brace of cousins was always handy, able, and willing to pass on the information. It was an arrangement which worked well, saving parents and teachers a lot of time and effort.

Cousins had their advantage, of course. You could depend upon them to rally around when the going got thick. In fact, there was a sort of code among us which decreed that we must fight our best friend, if necessary, for the sake of a cousin, twice removed, whom we didn't even like. Everyone in our town said it wasn't safe to say anything about anyone—with as many of us as there were, almost anybody mentioned would be our kin or kin to kin. And then, sure as anything, there'd be a good row.

Since Mama was the oldest, protocol demanded that the reunion of her family be held at our house. Accordingly they gathered on the appointed Sunday, each sister bringing enough food for the whole bunch, even if no one else provided a single crumb. They all carried their contributions to the kitchen and set about helping Mama while Grandma, easily the queen of them all, sat in the most comfortable rocking chair and visited with her daughters.

I must confess I preferred being in the kitchen where preparations were in progress rather than cruising around with the various visiting cousins. Listening to Mama and the aunts was as good as attending a play. Without being able to put the situation into words, I still knew the years had pushed back and these women —grown and with families—were once more girls at home, laughing and talking in a jargon which was a separate language of their own.

"I sent my washing to Mrs. Belden last week and it came back looking like Ethan Paxton's handkerchief." A great burst of laughter, quite beyond my comprehension. I had never heard of Ethan Paxton before, nor of his handkerchief. But to those laughing women, the reference was clear enough. And uproariously funny besides.

"'You can season the peas,'" Mama told a sister. "And *don't spare the butter!*"

Howls of mirth greeted this statement which, to me, was not funny at all. For goodness sakes, what was so hilarious about putting lots of butter in peas?

"I saw Dick Rutledge the other day."

That was the young man from Kansas City, supposed to be courting a distant cousin.

"Oh, you did. What does he look like?"

"Well—if he just had Kutch's eyes!"

So I knew at once there was some lack in the young man's appearance, not necessarily having to do with his eyes. The sisters all caught on fast enough, though; you could tell by the way they laughed.

Not a word about their own problems, which they undoubtedly had. Their children might be worrying them, or drought threatening the crops, or business lagging, or they themselves nursing some nagging pain or discomfort. Of these they did not speak. They were never women to parade their griefs.

Years later I was to see Helen Hayes in *The Wisteria Trees* and think with a puzzled sense of reincarnation that I had seen the play before. This I knew to be impossible, for although it was a version of *The Cherry Orchard,* still the play was new to Broadway.

"I always did say Mama had the right idea about mortgages," Miss Hayes declared. "She just ignored them."

Then I knew the reason back of my puzzlement. Once more I was in Mama's kitchen while she and her sisters talked in those thin, soft, light, slightly high-pitched voices of theirs, skirting all around their problems, laughing a great deal, flashing out with the quick burst of ridicule which, although keen, was never bitter or vindictive. Ignoring, figuratively speaking, the "mortgages" of life.

When I could tear myself away from the kitchen where all the excitement was going on, or in the afternoon after the magnificent meal had been consumed, I joined the other children in various activities. For the girls, building a playhouse was a favored pastime.

I think we would have scorned one of today's versions, which are nothing less than real houses built to scale. Ours was the wonderful world of make-believe, hemmed in by no boundaries save those of our imagination. Once we tried a tree house, but I fell out and broke my collarbone, so after that, by parental decree, we were earth-bound.

The best place for a playhouse is under an apple tree. Don't ask me to explain this—it is a premise which must be accepted on faith, just as one does not question that a rose is a rose. Sometimes we used bricks to mark off the outside limits or etch in the boundaries of the rooms. Once with more imagination than common sense, I decided it would be a great idea to stick willow saplings into the ground. These would grow, I assured the girl cousins who were assisting, thus forming a permanent playhouse. Accordingly, we all spent a busy afternoon cutting willow switches from the trees lining the creek at the foot of the hill. After we had anchored them in patterns we thought correct, we watered them so that they would start growing at once. This done, we sat down to rejoice in our accomplishment.

We reckoned without Papa. When he happened on to the scene of the wonderful playhouse, he took one look and gave the terse command.

"Pull them up!"

"Oh, Papa," I wailed in protest. "They will grow, and make such a nice playhouse."

"Yes," he agreed. "That's the trouble. They'll grow, all right. Like weeds. I don't intend to have a willow grove here in the orchard."

Realizing there was no appeal in this case, we pulled up the switches. I don't recall that we grieved over much. After all, if you set definite boundaries on your playhouse, you were handicapped if, all of a sudden, you decided to "p'like" (play like) it was a castle which reached to the very edge of the orchard.

Not only was the structure the project of our imagination, but the furnishings as well. Instead of real dishes, we had broken bits of china and crockery. These we washed and arranged with the same care bestowed by Mama on her prized heirlooms. Our stove was, in all likelihood, constructed from bricks; our table, a wooden box; our other furniture whipped up from odds and ends of junk. I remember watching carefully lest some young and irresponsible cousin disarrange our well-kept house.

What else did we do at reunions? Well, of course, we ate. Missouri cooking is, in itself, a gastronomical experience, and Mama and her sisters were equal to, if not better than, the other excellent cooks native to the state. Once the meal was finished there was the clearing away. And, of course, everybody talked. I sometimes maintain that I had to start writing because I was never, as a child, allowed to finish a sentence without being interrupted. You didn't wait your turn, or you would never have got a word in; you simply broke in when, and where, you could. With the cousins, that is. With adults, there was still the quaint idea in force that one didn't interrupt his elders. There were games, too—croquet and tennis and horseshoes and ones we made up for ourselves. But mostly the grownups talked. There were occasional variations—an aunt might "Give us a Reading"; a great-uncle could, and would upon occasion, recite pages from some book he was reading. I remember being introduced to *Les Miserables* at a family reunion. The great-uncle recited, from memory, pages of the book, using, as I have since discovered, phonetic pronunciation, anglicized for all proper names. Not having read the book at that time, I cannot vouch for the accuracy of his rendition.

Of course I know family reunions are still held, but I wonder how people manage. For one thing, how can you accommodate fifty or more people in an apartment or even in a split-level, three-bedroom model? It takes innumerable rooms—upstairs and down—to keep the children from under foot. You need a kitchen, big enough to hold the food the aunts brought and for the aunts who stay there to help with things. You need a screened-in back porch, running the full length of the house, with a couch and chairs and a table and an icebox. You need a croquet ground and a tennis court and a huge shady yard, front, sides and back, to congregate in. It is better if there is a barn loft, filled with hay, and an orchard. And, of course, trees to climb and horses to ride and dogs to follow, yipping wildly, every move the children make.

In short, the ingredients for a successful family reunion are not so simple as they sound. One needs vastly more than just the kin.

I would not try to leave the impression that at such gatherings, all was sweetness and light. Times were when, as Mama put it, "The fur flew." Mama's family were mostly Irish, given to quick tears and quick tempers as well as quick laughter. The children were not noted for their lovely dispositions, nor were the adults a bit above tossing a few hasty words back and forth. But these spells never lasted long and, like as not, we would suspend our minor differences to gather around the piano and sing the old songs, with Aunt Gertrude, the musical aunt, leading us, our voices breaking now and then at the sentimental points.

The word for such stuff now is "corny"; we thought it was utterly lovely.

Not long ago a cousin, separated by miles from the place we knew as children (as I am separated, as most of the others are), said to me, "Do you suppose it was really as wonderful as we remember it?"

And I said, "Of course it wasn't. That is the magic of it all."

And so it is. Down the years we have been able to turn loose the evil, hold fast to the good, a mental process for which we have Biblical authority. Within our hearts we have built up our oases of memory, misty as a Corot or Monet painting. It is as ridiculous to say that Corot should be a Grant Wood as it is to insist that we reject our own idealistic view of reunions.

Time was when we were a clan in the community. At intervals, sometimes in sequence and sometimes concurrently, Papa was superintendent of Sunday school, Mama and various aunts were teaching classes, Aunt Meta played the piano, and Grandpa was a steward in the church. It is not a bad thing, this clan business. The strength it offers, the solidarity, the pride. The feeling of being a part of something bigger and stronger than oneself. The need for loyalty. Even, perhaps, the chance to work off steam in your own private fights.

Not only were Mama's people Irish, they also had a bit of Scotch in them with the right to wear the Bruce plaid. Somewhere I had read that Queen Elizabeth II was, on her mother's side, also descended from this brave Scotsman. When I went to Europe, I vowed I was a good mind to drop by Buckingham Palace and say, "See here, Cousin Elizabeth, back in Missouri, where I grew up, kinfolk stick together. How's about putting me up while I'm visiting here?"

And so we did, and so we do.

Last year our family tried another reunion, to help Aunt Frances and Uncle Ben celebrate their Golden Wedding Anniversary. We flew in to Kansas City from all points of the compass, and from there went on to the scene of the reunion, meekly enough, on buses. We came in cars and we came on trains. We walked across the street. The main thing was, we got there. We kissed everybody in sight. (The story is that I kissed three perfectly strange men, not sure of how cousins had changed in the years since last I saw them. For goodness sakes, you don't want to hurt anybody's feelings at such a time.) We hugged each other, and we all talked at once, and we cried a little and we laughed a lot. And, of course, we ate and ate.

It was fascinating to watch the reunions within the reunions. Sisters who hadn't seen each other for all of two weeks would fly out to meet a newly arrived sister. You'd think they had been separated from birth, kept apart by a cruel stepmother or a wicked witch, starved for news of one another. The kissing and the hugging and the oh-ing and ah-ing that went on were something to watch.

Then all the rest of us gathered around and said, "Oh my, you look wonderful—you get younger and prettier every day you live." We followed that with, "You haven't changed a bit!"

Funny thing, we meant every word we said.

When I was on the small side, I was sure I knew exactly what heaven would be like. The vision came to me as the lot of us sat in church one Sunday morning singing the words,

"Thus may all our Sabbaths prove
Till we join the church above."

It would be a place where Mama and Papa and the kin to the farthest degree, including in-laws and kin to kin, would be gathered. Whenever a new family angel came, we would rush to the gates to meet him (so he wouldn't feel lonesome or strange) and tell him how wonderful he looked and how glad we were to see him. Then we would settle down to our harps and some good group singing.

Across the years I look back at her now, the little girl sitting there in her church pew, trying hard not to be vain about the flowers on her new hat, and I cannot find it in my heart to laugh at her. Perhaps she was right, in some way my knowledge is too limited to understand. In fact, I hope she was.

It sounds rather lovely to me.

VIII.

We Did It for the Town

THE season was nicely balanced between summer and fall. The rush of spring's plowing and planting was over; the richness of autumn's harvest was, as yet, no more than a satisfying promise. Gardens and frying chickens were at their best. And so were we—mellow, pleased with ourselves and our endeavors, hopeful and ambitious for the future.

The time was a natural for the Chautauqua.

The men who brought the Chautauqua to us in those golden years—the teens and early twenties—doubtless realized this and, with nice timing and a fine flair for shownmanship, flung their tents across the continent to bring us a variety of entertainment, the like of which we would otherwise not have known. A giant rose and fell in those days, and we were both witness and contributor to the phenomenon.

This we did not realize at the time or, knowing, didn't give a hoot. Our awareness was of a more personal nature. We knew Chautauqua combined the excitement of the circus with the unquestioned respectability of church. The ordinary Sunday night service, like the rounds of the New York postmen, could be stayed by no condition of wind or weather. But when Chautauqua came to town, the ministers not only dismissed their congregations but also went themselves. If ever a deacon or elder protested the mass exodus, the complaint was not made a matter of record.

Parents, too, looked favorably upon the Chautauqua. They

might frown on tent shows as being of the Stage and, therefore, having some sort of loose connection, vague but certain, with sin. They also professed horror at some of the ideas movies could well put into young heads. But for Chautauqua, with its week-long program of music, lectures, and plays, they had nothing but approval. I don't know why a play on the Chautauqua stage seemed more moral than one a stock company put on. Maybe it was because the actors in the former always looked more prosperous and didn't wear so much make-up. Of course, there was always an American flag on one side of the platform, and people naturally wouldn't want to put on a shoddy performance under those conditions.

Probably this ready endorsement came, in a way, because the institution belonged to the town. True, the talent was from afar, sent to us by men we did not know, through agents whom we saw rarely, if at all. Even so, the Chautauqua was ours because we paid for it. In advance with a guarantee that the necessary money would be in the bank before the opening day, a contract signed by responsible people of the town. We whose fathers were members of this civic-minded group invariably exhibited a certain smug pride over the matter. For a few days after the signing, I regret to say, we were apt to be self-righteous and, probably, thoroughly despised by those children whose parents did not lean so heavily toward philanthropy. It was a smugness without justification, for usually the Chautauqua paid off.

It could not well fail to do so because, since it was our own, we supported it as we did the high school basketball team, the city park, or the annual Fourth of July picnic. It was also our opera, our theater, our lecture platform. It was the artery through which the pulse of the world beat, and once a year we were privileged to take the count with our very own fingers.

We would have missed our chance at heaven with scarcely less dismay than we would have given up, willingly, the privilege of seeing the week-long series of programs, afternoon and evening. Partly this was because we all had season tickets and were cannily bent on getting our money's worth. But mainly we were interested in the programs, which were good and different from anything we had a chance to see elsewhere. Moreover, Chautauqua was synonymous with vacation week, ideal because it came to us rather than demanding that we go to it. We sat back with the pleased complacency of a king who has just summoned his chief jester and sees that he is responding in top form.

For the world of entertainment did come to us, and in the flesh. We had read in books about people who were different from us, but the knowledge was largely academic. For my part, reality was brought home to me by Miss Kitty Malone, a maiden lady in town, who kept boarders. One afternoon during Chautauqua week a group of dark-skinned people came to her front door, asking if they might make arrangements to eat their meals with her while they were in town. She took one look at them, stiffened her spine, and told them her table was full.

"The very idea," she said indignantly, not bothering to shut the door before she spoke. "Negroes, wanting me to feed them with my other guests."

Slowly the leader of the group turned, came back to the door where Miss Kitty still stood.

"Madam," he said, "we are Hawaiians, here to play at the Chautauqua this evening. But even if we were Negroes, what difference could it make, so long as we are hungry?"

Miss Kitty refused to go to the Chautauqua that evening, the only person in the community so minded. We couldn't get enough of the Hawaiians as they sang and played their guitars, their music breaking over us in waves of delicate sadness.

I listened, remembering Miss Kitty and her refusal to feed these wonderful people. Before today, it had never occurred to me to question anything she said; even her prejudices seemed right and proper. Now conviction stirred in me. Miss Kitty had been wrong to treat them as she did. After all, what difference did their color make if they were hungry? We were hungry for music, and they did not refuse us simply because we were of a different color and from a different land.

In one thundering second of revelation the map of the world came alive for me. The people who lived in those faraway places walked and talked and knew hunger and happiness and fear, even as we did. I'd never look at a map again without an awareness that those green and pink and blue splotches represented more than mere divisions of countries; they were the homes of people who, probably, were a great deal like us.

The world came to us in other, more romantic ways.

The men who managed the Chautauqua were smart enough to know that if they could line up the organization with the approval of education and the church, they could brag of it as being uplift all the way. So, they selected not only the performers but the personnel with this in mind. Even the traveling crew who went ahead to put up tents and take care of details was made up of young men of good character, usually working their way through college. Frequently, some of the performers also were college boys, amateurs trying their hand at entertaining. Particularly was this true of the male quartets, always extremely popular with us. Their pictures were sent ahead, showing them to be almost too handsome to move among ordinary mortals.

There was always a concentration of girls—the pretty, young, unmarried ones—at these programs. They sat down front, wearing their best clothes and flirting outrageously with the performers. It was a wonder we ever got any sort of program out of the quartet at all. Perhaps they were used to this, although I am sure it never failed to flatter them. Perhaps, because of this coterie of admirers sitting there so close to them, they did even better than they might have otherwise. I think that was our general attitude, for we smiled indulgently, even when the boys seemed to be singling out individual girls toward whom they directed the more romantic portions of their songs.

There were some who did not take the matter so well. The local boys, especially those who felt their own special girls were carrying things too far even for the sake of inspiring a Chautauqua performer, sat glowering, sometimes refusing to clap when the number was finished. Nobody missed their sound of approval, however—we clapped our hands until they were worn out and brought the singers back until they finally said they just didn't have another number to give us. Then they'd sign off with "Drink To Me Only With Thine Eyes," making every girl in the front row feel the invitation was directed to her alone. This done, they'd go off the stage, get immediately into their automobile, and take off for the next town where they were scheduled to appear.

Strangely enough, I don't believe it ever occurred to us to give a reception for them after the performance, or to invite them to have dinner with us, or make any effort to have them step out of their roles as performers. We accepted them for what they were and perhaps, even unconsciously, did not wish to see behind the façade.

We did, however, have our own brand of social activity during the week. It was a great time for our friends to say, "There's no need to go home between sessions—just stay and have supper with us." Or, a group would decide—over the telephone on the morning of the performance—that they'd all bring a picnic lunch and eat in the grove back of the tent. "I'll bring fried chicken," Mama would volunteer, and they'd plan from there. Those suppers, eaten on the Chautauqua ground, with the white tent in the background and the promise of entertainment to come, still stand out in my mind. After we had eaten, we children would play, but not long and certainly no strenuous games, for after all, we had to keep ourselves clean for the evening performance.

Not all of our programs were music. Sometimes there was a Chalk Talk. I suspected the artist speaker of talking only to prevent us from watching the drawing or of drawing to keep our minds off what he was saying. I determined to watch instead of listen (there being some flaw in my powers of comprehension which made it impossible for me to do both simultaneously) in order to see what he was up to. The performer I selected to make my test on drew something resembling a wall with smoke curling over it, adding some clouds and flowers. I was following him with unblinking concentration when suddenly he upended the picture, a move I considered downright unsportsmanlike of him, and there was the Statue of Liberty. At that precise moment a woman (who had slipped to the piano unnoticed) struck up "The Star-Spangled Banner" and everyone, as if by previous arrangement, stood and began to sing. Except me. I felt I had been betrayed by a cheap trick, and I didn't mean to let out one faint peep even if Mama did take me to task afterwards for not joining in the National Anthem.

Financing the Chautauqua was no problem at all in good years, but in times of drought or crop failure things did not go so easily. I remember one of those bad years when drought sat heavily on the land, ruining any hope we might have had for the crops. It was at this time that the advance leaflet announced a lecture on "The Millionaire of Uz."

We at once jumped to the conclusion that we would hear a thorough castigation of Wall Street, the whipping boy of all our rural minds. To this villain we could ascribe most of our troubles. Without actually saying so, we even harbored a dim suspicion that the drought could be laid at its door. Most assuredly Wall Street might be blamed. The Lord was punishing the men there by withholding the rain which would make the crops on which they gambled. It was a great relief to be able to isolate the reason for our hard times. The lecture had a promising sound; we looked forward to a satisfying evening of exorcising the Devil.

But Papa, himself a Bible student, got that notion out of our heads. The Millionaire of Uz, he told us, was Job, the patient, long-suffering man in the Bible. So, of course, we weren't surprised that the minister dismissed evening service and urged us all to go hear the speaker.

We knew about Job ahead of time. He was a farmer, like so many of our friends and neighbors. He was a good man, and loved his family, even as the men we knew. He was having a hard time; so were we, in that difficult summer. In fact, I had the secret feeling that the Lord had been a bit unfair to Job, a good man and his servant, just as he was being a shade unfair to the good men in our community. I went to the lecture mentally daring the speaker to justify Job's plight.

He did not fail me. Nor the audience either, who I suspect, had shared my resentment without quite daring to express it.

No ordinary lecture, this. Here, as the speaker talked to us in words we could understand, evolved the parable of man's long struggle against the forces of evil, disappointment, suffering, and despair. These were not new things, invented by Wall Street for our confoundment. Evil was ancient and insidious, and there was no sure way of fixing the blame for it. There were times when all man could do about it was to face his problem with courage and faith. Moreover, goodness did finally triumph, some-times in a way we did not recognize, often at times long delayed.

We needed much to hear these things. Afterwards, we went out into the hot dry night feeling a little more confident of our ability to cope with drought, the forces of evil, life, and even Wall Street.

It is not strange that this man whose name has long since been forgotten by us who heard him was able to talk so convincingly. The Chautauqua lectures were one of the strongest features of the entire program. Many of the most famous speakers of the time, men and women alike, found their way to the platform. Foremost among them, of course, was William Jennings Bryan.

They called him the Silver Tongued Orator, and rightly so. Even now it is pretty well conceded that he was one of the greatest speakers of all time. He had only to open his mouth and let the first bell-like syllables roll out in order to make the audience his, a state in which it remained for any length of time he chose to speak. It did not matter how hard the seats, how hot the tent. No one would deny, either, that it was possible to listen to him, be enthralled by him, and come away with only the haziest notion of what he had said.

He was a bit too big to come to our Chautauqua, which after all, was financed by a small town and a rural community. When I finally had my chance to hear him, later when I was at the age where I thought myself older than I shall ever feel again, I passed up the opportunity. I had gone with a group to a Sunday school convention in Kansas City, quite properly chaperoned—oh, my goodness yes! But our chaperone must have been either lax or light-minded, or maybe she just deliberately shut her eyes to the mutiny which developed in her ranks. At any rate, several of us —boys and girls—decided we didn't want to hear that old man anyway. He was sure to be boring. So we went instead to Swope Park for the evening.

We had a wonderful time, riding everything that moved at all, had our fortunes told, and felt pleasantly sinful and wonderfully daring. But I did not get off entirely free. Although I read the account of Bryan's talk next morning in the *Times* and could give a proper account of it once I was home, I never really came out and confessed that I didn't go. Oh, I didn't say I went— that would have been lying. For months afterwards whenever Bryan's name came up I was nervous and uneasy. And when, a few years later, the Great Commoner went down to ignoble defeat at the hands of Darrow, I felt a sense of responsibility. For had I not rejected him first? It was almost as if I had been the initial pebble in the avalanche of public repudiation which poured over the great man and which, some insisted, was the cause of his death.

Year after year we gathered at the Chautauqua tent to listen to them—the lecturers, the yodelers, the bell-ringers, the girl who sat behind her harp, not only looking, but playing, like an angel peering through the bars of heaven. Some of the performers, like the Hawaiians, came from distant lands. Scientists came, and men who knew the world from having traveled in it, and ministers and teachers and statesmen (these last-named usually past their prime). Actors brought their world of make-believe which, for a time, became more real than our own.

They stayed with us briefly, but when they went away, they left something of themselves with us; and, for all I know, maybe they took something of us with them. We saw them go, knowing that in all likelihood, we would never see them again. We did not need to. For they were leaving us as custodians of the truth they spread. We were a whole nation, linked in the nurture of truth. That gave us a feeling of responsibility beyond mere pleasure. We must see that Chautauqua came back to us next year.

That was why, on the last night when the college-boy crew had taken the tent down and the next year's sponsors had been announced and the bit of land which had housed the Chautauqua had become once more a pasture at the edge of town, a feeling of virtue flooded our souls. We had assured for the town the best gift we knew how to give. And we had a confidence, dimly realized but nonetheless sure, that in direct proportion to the way we strengthened our town—by our own efforts and in our own way—we were strengthening the nation. Maybe even the world, for all we knew.

But of that we did not speak as we drove home, we children half asleep, drowsy, and content. Mama said to Papa, "It was good. I think the best we've ever had."

"You say that every year," Papa teased her.

"I do, and I'm right," Mama defended herself.

And so she was.

Fall

IX.

Feet That Went to School

FOR the most part, anything I read in a book was gospel truth. There was one point, however, at which I took issue with the printed page and that was where Mr. Whittier talked about feet creeping slow to school. I loved school and couldn't imagine anyone failing to share my sentiments.

At our place preparations started early in August when Miss Mattie arrived to do the fall sewing. Sister and I were to get three new dresses each, the theory being that these, together with the ones left over from the previous year, would be sufficient wardrobe to see us through until spring and the return of Miss Mattie. In the early years, she also made little articles of apparel called blouses for Brother, but he quickly graduated to shirts bought at the store.

It was also necessary to buy new dinner pails. Some children used tin syrup buckets, but I believe we thought ourselves above such a practice. Brown in color, rectangular in shape, ours were made from a super-strong brand of cardboard which we fondly believed could not be distinguished from leather. There was a real leather strap across the top. The box itself was a part of all that it had ever met in the way of food, since there was no real way of washing out the flimsy receptacle. Even so, there were careful children who managed to use theirs for two years or even longer. We did not belong to that select group.

On the same trip, we bought school supplies—pencils, pens,

ink, crayons, paper, and books. This being before the day of free textbooks, it was up to us to provide our own tools of learning. Usually I had to buy new water colors as well, for I was an uninhibited soul given to using color with abandon. As a result, my art education must have been seriously lopsided, since by the time spring and the season for painting tulips had come, I was completely out of reds and yellows and so had to be satisfied with doing leafless trees, making use of the left-over browns. It never occurred to me to ask Mama and Papa to buy me another set of colors; I am sure the request would have been granted after a little lecture on "Waste not, want not," but the rule was one box per pupil per year, and I was not one to go against custom. I went ahead drawing brown *objets d'art,* and so far as I have been able to see, it caused no permanent kink in my personality. Mostly I learned I'd better make do with what I had and that, figuratively speaking, I couldn't have my cake and eat it, too.

Literally this adage about the cake was true as well. Mama sent our lunch with us each day, packed in that brown cardboard lunch box. Once we set out for school, things were strictly up to us. The food was there for us to eat; we could make up our minds as to the time. Obviously, noon was the most logical hour, but if we happened to be hungry at morning recess, there was no law saying we couldn't eat then. The decision involved some weighing and balancing, for we knew we couldn't have our lunch both times. Mama usually packed a special treat to tide us over recess, but still the temptation was always there —ours to meet and either conquer or embrace. With no outside help, we were left to make the decision as an adult would do.

In fact, school was a pretty fair sample of what the adult world was like. Here we were a part of a continuing society, being thrown each day with people both younger and older than ourselves. We played together on a common playground, often the same games, a forbearance brought about not so much by magnanimity as by the necessity for having enough players for the game. The younger ones learned not to ask any favors, because even though they might be included, they were not necessarily welcome. Under these conditions, though, the older ones developed a sense of responsibility and the young ones grew up fast.

Witness Brother. He was a beautiful youngster, with blue eyes, curly hair and pink cheeks. He was, likewise, the baby in the family and, as such, mourned by Mama when time came for him to go to school. Sensing this, he was affronted, just as he was unhappy because Mama sent him to school, on that first all-important day, wearing a summer suit—linen pants buttoned to a blouse. She gave as her excuse the unseasonable warmth of September and the fact that by next year he would outgrow the outfit.

Brother knew quite well this situation must be met with firmness if he were to gain acceptance among the Big Boys. Leaving Sister and me, he made his way over to join his heroes.

Once among them, he looked at a tall lanky boy named Silas Brown, who was wearing a pair of shoes which had either been carried over from another era or bought by his thrifty mother at a bargain table. At any rate, Brother had never seen their like before.

Brother saw what he believed to be his chance. Squaring off, he spat with sufficient vigor as to almost clear his baby chin. "—— —— ——, Silas," he said. "Where'd you get them shoes?"

Sister and I stood frozen in our tracks, expecting that we'd have to leave school or maybe even move out of the neighborhood once news of Brother's depravity got around. Not only had he sworn an oath but he had used bad grammar as well. Of course it would be our duty to tell Mama, although our hearts were not in it.

Mama did not react to the information in quite the way we had anticipated. True, she reprimanded Brother, but it looked to me as if she was trying hard not to smile as she did so. The next day he did not wear the linen suit. Whatever version Papa received of the incident was given in private. I am sure he had a little talk, also private, with Brother. Both he and Mama knew without doubt that if we were to get along in school, we had to make a place for ourselves. There was no counselor to advise us on our correct relations with the group and no psychiatrist to scare the living daylights out of our parents in case those relations went awry. The responsibility was strictly our own, a situation which we were sometimes reluctant to recognize. In my case, at any rate.

Aunt Lucy was teaching our school at that time. She had the job because Papa was on the school board. (We had never heard of antinepotism in our community, would have given it scant heed had we known about it. How else would the school get desirable teachers if we couldn't depend on the kin of the board members!) I had said something about one of the girls which hurt her feelings deeply—I don't remember whether I questioned her honesty or spoke disparagingly of her new dress. Whatever it was, my words sent her to my teacher-aunt who listened to the report and then called me to her.

"You will have to apologize," she ruled, once she had made certain of my guilt in the matter.

I knew the voice of authority when I heard it. "All right," I agreed. "Call her over here and I'll do it."

I didn't sound very repentant, even to my own ears.

"Oh, no," my aunt said. "You must go to her."

"But she's with a whole bunch of kids," I protested. "I can't apologize with all of them listening."

"You said it before them, didn't you?" she reminded me.

I pondered her words. I looked at the inflexible face of authority. I looked at the children—the big ones, the little ones, and those between, the ones who were my own age. They were watching me, knowing something out of the ordinary was in the air. I swallowed two or three times.

"Might as well get it over with," my aunt advised sensibly.

I hesitated only a moment longer. Then I turned and marched over to where the injured girl stood. I do not remember what I said to her, but it must have been adequate, for she mumbled something which sounded like "Oh, that's all right." Those who heard must have shared her sentiments, for they got out of the tight little knot into which they had been bound and started a baseball game. I was chosen third or fourth instead of the usual well-toward-the-last, for at baseball I was no good at all. I never seemed to see the ball until it was well past me.

I wish I could say I was a model child after that and learned to control my tongue. Not me. But something started inside my mind and heart that day which was to remain within me. A feeling of individual responsibility for my actions and the knowledge that public accusation demands public retraction.

Or should, at any rate.

The school was set on a largish plot of ground with trees and a well. It was the duty of the big boys to pump water and put it on the shelf in the anteroom, where we kept our lunch boxes and our wraps. There was a common drinking dipper, but Mama bought each of us a small, collapsible drinking cup. I often lost mine and had to borrow from Sister. I think Brother would have died of thirst before he would have asked the loan of one of our cups.

Two small buildings sat discreetly apart from each other and from the school building. There were no names on either one, but it was the duty of the older students to take you aside on your first day and explain which was which. There was an enormous playground where we played together with little or no supervision and certainly no suggestion as to what we should play. But baseball was the favorite.

Once we had an invitation to play a town team, an honor which came to us because our teacher of the year, a man, lived in town and told some friends what a good bunch of players he had. He should have kept his mouth shut, for upon taking count of his forces, he discovered that no matter how he worked it, there were only seven boys big enough to hold a bat. So we did what reason dictated. We decided to take two girls along in order to make up the team.

Sister was the first one chosen. No great shakes at batting, she was nevertheless a good sport and usually kept her head in emergencies. Moreover, she could run like a startled gazelle. Another girl who could be depended upon was chosen, and, like the armies of France setting out with the Maid of Orleans at their head, we took off for town. It would be good to say that the two maidens so chosen were modest and sweet and unaware of their importance. This I cannot in good conscience report. They queened it over us all, and the boys would not have endured their presence for a minute had they not been necessary to the game.

The sight of a team with two girls members sent the town boys into fits of laughter. When Sister stood up to bat, the pitcher threw the ball with an exaggerated overhead motion, mimicking a girl. At the same time, all the fielders ran back, calling to each other to be ready for a long ball. They were in no way prepared for the thing that did happen.

Sister hit the ball. It landed only a few feet from home plate, but even so, it was a fair ball. Before a single boy could recover enough to run in from his outlying post, Sister was off to first. She made it, trailed by the ball which arrived a split second after she did. The first baseman, overcome by the sight of the streak of skirts whirling past him, missed the ball. By the time he retrieved and threw to second, she was away and gone, on her way to third. Shaken and unbelieving, the boy on second base also missed. By this time, anybody could see what was going to happen. Sister, the ball following her like a satellite, came racing in for the team's one home run.

The effect on the rival team was one of complete demoralization. We won, hands down. It would be nice to give a sequel to this story, a pretty little tribute in which Sister was publicly proclaimed as a heroine, savior of the day. The boys, as a matter of fact, barely mentioned the incident. For goodness sakes, if a couple of silly girls had to go along, they ought to show some gratitude by performing well.

What equipment we had we furnished ourselves. The Big Boys brought bats and balls from home, a gesture not inspired by pure philanthropy. The possessor of such prestige items was sure to have a place in the game, perhaps even to be declared captain. Not only did we furnish our own equipment, we often made up our own rules and, it must be confessed, not infrequently changed them as we went along, a process which may have added to our ingenuity and most certainly contributed to our arguments.

We played Blackman, of course. Here it was the unwritten code that the Big Boys must always, at least once in every play period, take-through some smaller child. I remember to this day the intense delight which came of flying across the ground, my hand held fast in the great paw of one of the elect, racing to the goal I was confident of reaching thus escorted. I am sure etiquette demanded that the Big Boys so encumbered should pass through safely; at the time, however, I was aware only of a great and perfect confidence, a special watchful care. So the Children of Israel must have felt, passing dry-shod across the Red Sea.

Pretty soon the teacher rang the bell, and we went inside.

Teacher sat on a platform, authority enthroned. We went up to him—or to her, as the case might be, although it so happens that most of my teachers were men. We went when we were called, and we sat on a bench facing teacher, our backs to the others. The theory was that we were supposed to study our own lessons while the other classes were reciting. Actually, we listened in, an earlier version of educational television, and thus it was that our triumphs and our downfalls became matters of public interest.

In town, where Papa had his business and Grandma and Grandpa lived and we went to church, there was a concentration of Mama's people. But the country school, as it were, was descended from Papa's side of the house. Papa's father had helped to found it and had been clerk and director; here Papa and his sisters and brothers had attended school. Later, when Papa himself became the head of a family he inherited his father's place as clerk and, at intervals, director. (The name we gave to

our school board members.) I still have in my possession the
books in which the minutes were kept, written first in Grandfather's precise, steel-engraving handwriting and later in Papa's
own distinctive scrawl. They hold the record of a community—
so much coal bought, so much paid a man for cleaning out the
well, so much for repairs, and such and such salaries paid to
teachers. (Sums which would bring either smiles of derision or
snorts of unbelief from educators now.) If one wanted to, he
could reconstruct a community and an era, just reading the
simple cryptic words recorded in those books.

When I read them, as I have upon rare occasions, I always feel
anew that it is a good thing for families to live out their lives in
one community, to set their stamp upon it, and to have, in turn, it
set its stamp upon them.

We were not without a cousin in this school, a boy, kin to
us on Papa's side. He was, moreover, in my class and, alas, far
smarter than I. Perhaps that is why I still remember the only
time I was able to spell him down. I must report the contest
was not entirely fair. He had first try at the word and missed, so
of course when it came to me I knew to spell it the other way.
Because I have a mean streak in me, I have not forgotten; the
chances are he still may remember, too, since that was the only
time it happened.

The school was, in due time, to disappear, to consolidate with
a town school, even before Brother finished. But when I was
there the winds of change had not yet hit us, and we still had all
grades in one room, taught by one teacher. Recognizing very
sensibly that he could not be all things to all pupils, he initiated
on his own a system of teacher aides. One of the large girls was
sent to the cloakroom with the smaller children, there to give us
our spelling, listen to our multiplication tables, and, upon occasion, hear us read. For the most part it worked out fine. The
only trouble in my case was that Kate Harper, the monitor I
most often drew, had a crush on a Big Boy who sat next to the
anteroom door. She never heard a word I said, of that I am
convinced. I could, and probably did, get my i's and e's trans-

posed and tripped ingloriously over my tables, without her ever catching me. But perhaps the end result was on the plus side. Teacher's sanity was saved, Kate eventually captured the Big Boy and together they settled down to make a good home, and I learned to look up every doubtful word in the dictionary. (What I do in matters touching on math is my own business.)

Teachers also faced very sensibly a situation which educators are just now recognizing. A child cannot always be placed in the exact grade where he belongs, since it is quite possible, for one reason or another, that he may do his arithmetic at a fourth grade level, read with the eighth graders, and have a preprimary ability in art. My own uneven development in this respect came about because I sat listening while the older boys and girls recited history and English and geography until I felt I could have taken the place of any of them, as an understudy standing in the wings knows she could do the leading lady's part on a moment's notice.

My seventh grade teacher was not unaware of this. So, the day he gave the county examinations to the eighth graders he looked at me, watching wide-eyed and alert as he opened the envelope containing the questions, and said, "There's an extra set of questions. Why don't you try your hand at answering them? Just for experience—then you'll know how to go about it next year when your turn comes?"

I took the questions he handed me without one single misgiving. Hadn't I read every page of the Elson Readers, not only mine but the eighth grade ones as well? Hadn't I devoured every book in the school library, not once but several times? Hadn't I pored over history books, both at home and at school? And, most convincing of all, hadn't I sat and listened to the eighth graders recite until their mistakes were as familiar to me as were my own? Besides, there was no occasion for concern—this was just a trial run.

The unbelievable thing was that I passed and went on to high school a year ahead of myself. I will never believe that the authorities at the county seat (from whence came the questions and to whom the papers were sent for grading) really read my arithmetic paper. (I always studied my own lessons while the arithmetic classes recited.) Nor do I think they took off for misspelling. But most remarkable of all nobody questioned Teacher's right to give the examination to a pupil who was technically not entitled to take it.

Whatever our teacher might have lacked—adequate salary, teaching aids, approved teaching load—he certainly did possess, in full measure, standing in the community. He made his own decisions, backing them with his own authority. He was looked up to as a person of substance and worth. One of the biggest occasions in the school calendar was the time Teacher came home to spend the night with you. The dinner Mama cooked to do honor to the occasion was every bit as delectable as the one prepared for the preacher. Promptly upon arriving home from school, we put on our best clothes and then helped Mama set the table with the Haviland china, the cut glass, and the good silver. Moreover, we knew only the best manners were acceptable at such times, and we'd better remember them.

We worked ourselves into a fine glow over the whole affair. It lasted through the next day when we opened our lunch boxes with the pleasant knowledge that Teacher's box contained a duplicate meal. Usually Teacher, under the mellowing influence of the good food, would treat us with a special indulgence we found highly gratifying. But for two things we might have become insufferable. First, Teacher apparently forgot all about his visit by the next day. Second, the other children were not disposed to allow us any delusions of grandeur. After all, Teacher would go home with all of them before the year was over, and each one would have his place in the sun.

So we lived each day to the hilt, never once realizing that before too many years the sort of school we were attending would be almost as extinct as the passenger pigeon, just as we never stopped to think it was as American as hot dogs and apple pie.

But even had we known, we probably would have shown scant interest. We would have been more concerned with choosing up sides and taking time for one more quick go at baseball before the bell rang.

X.

"The House Will Come to Order—"

THERE were times when I thought the grownups were as anxious as I was for fall and the opening of school, although for quite a different reason. This was the season of the Literary Society, a thoroughly adult organization in which we children were allowed only minor roles.

The members of the community waited for school to settle into its routine and for the teacher, if he was new, to get the hang of things. Since four weeks was considered a proper period of grace, the date for the opening meeting was usually set for the first week in October.

Naturally, every child was on hand, as well as all the able-bodied adults of the community, with a sense of excitement hanging over everything. At the appointed hour, Teacher would walk to his desk, rap for attention, and say, "The house will now come to order."

Whereupon the buzz of conversation would die and then we knew we were off on another year of pleasure and delight.

This first meeting was primarily for organizational purposes. A president, vice-president, and secretary were elected. There was no treasurer. In this Utopian group we had no money, nor yet the need for it. The new president then stepped forward to take charge and initiated a catch-as-catch-can program. Sometimes this would be group singing or recitations. Here we children came into our own, for we were sure to be about the only ones who could be counted on with such short notice. I recall Sister and I once sang a song we had learned from listening to it being played on one of our own victrola records. We acted so smug and proud it was a wonder our fellow pupils didn't throw us out on our ears. Once the smart boy cousin gave, with considerable drama and much sentiment, "Horatius at the Bridge," a piece he had memorized from our reader for Friday afternoon recitations. Hearing him, I felt goose pimples pop out all over me. I forgave him for being smarter than I was and immediately set about learning the piece for myself.

I think it was Mama's secret—and great—hope that some time I would be able to play for the group at one of those early, impromptu programs. Alas, this ambition was never to be realized. Papa bought us a piano and I "took" for a couple of years, but lacked the will or the spark, or some other ingredient, necessary to a musician. I did learn to play a few simple melodies, so that I could accompany family singsongs, although I must confess that usually I followed the singers rather than the other way around. Actually I raced along, trying to keep up, for all the world like a child being pulled by his elders at a pace much too fast for him.

The regular meetings of the Literary Society were taken more seriously, with a committee planning ahead. One of the most exciting evenings came when we had debates, with the able speakers of the community taking sides and arguing back and forth while we all listened intently. For days afterward we discussed these debates and the decision of the judges with which, of course, we did not always agree. There was no shortage of talent, for our organization was well and favorably known, even upon occasion drawing speakers from adjoining communities. I can still remember some of the issues discussed, recall the organization of the debaters' speeches, the swift and telling rebuttal.

Naturally, we children were never allowed to participate in

so important a part of the program. This was adult business, serious and deep. But we did occasionally get in on another phase, the annual play given by the drama-minded members. For this everyone worked together, making props, contriving costumes, and designing sets, all with considerable verve and imagination—an earlier version of the Little Theater or Community Players. Of course, if the play selected had parts for children, we were chosen without question, or at least, such of us as displayed some talent.

I remember once we staged a tear-jerker with Sister cast as the small child abandoned in the snow by a cruel set of parents. I believe her father was out on the town, or something, and her foolish mother had sent her in search of him. Anyway, whatever the reason, she wound up sitting alone and desperate, freezing to death in the snow while she sang a plaintive little song about her plight. It never occurred to us that any child with a grain of intelligence would have more properly used her energy in going to the first door she saw, knocking, and then asking to be taken home. Instead she sat down and sang, and we were supposed to throw simulated snow on her as we stood concealed in the wings.

We made the snow by tearing up bits of newspaper very finely. At first we experimented with tissue paper, which was undeniably whiter but did not fall so well. Likewise we discarded the idea of cutting the paper in favor of tearing since, after all, snowflakes were uneven in shape and irregular in size. Finally we had a truly formidable cache of pseudo-snow in a box on the platform and we could go back to the study of such humdrum stuff as grammar and arithmetic.

Came the night of the play. Came the moment of the snowstorm. Sister, ragged and shivering (from excitement those shivers came, but real as if she were actually freezing), sat on the edge of the stage while a cohort and I stood in the wings with instructions to pelt the poor child with snow.

We threw the first tentative handful. The effect was truly wonderful. We grew bolder, and a great flurry of snow descended. Sister started her song, her small voice bewailing her fate. It was too much for me. So real the whole business was, I broke into tears and stopped my snow-throwing, unable to add to the sum of her misery. With a disgusted look in my direction, my companion went about her work, throwing larger handfuls in order to overcome my failure. Even so, the scene came off with little more than half a snowstorm.

Not long ago a group of us went to see *La Bohème*. The cast was polished, the stage setting beautiful, the actors in full voice. But the snow, quite obviously, was artificial. Sister, sitting beside me, was evidently thinking the same thing. Once outside she said, "We did it better, back at Catron School."

Our levity disgusted the others in the party, but we knew we were right. The snow here *was* artificial. There was no way of making us believe in it, or that the heroine was really cold or actually dying. The whole thing was opera, well-acted, well-sung, but make-believe. We lived our plays. Imagination took over so that, for a little while, we were in the world peopled by the characters, more real than the people before whom we said our lines. To this day I don't want anyone to tell me my hands didn't actually get cold from throwing that snow. It was as real as my unwillingness to add to Sister's misery.

It was a wonder we didn't all come down with pneumonia afterward.

Once we even wrote our own play. It must have been utterly impossible as far as creative excellence was concerned. But it did have a value in that every child had something to say.

Of course, we were a haven for politicians, and in election year they came in bunches, like bananas. Our Literary Society was the only one for miles around, so they considered us their natural sounding board. They came and shook hands and kissed babies, naturally, and talked brightly with the women and flirted a little—not too much, for after all, there was no sense in offending any voter—with the girls. And then they got up on the platform and told us how wonderful we were, the salt of the earth, the real defenders of democracy, the solid substantial roots on which this country was built. We already were a shade on the complacent side, so I doubt that the talks influenced us one way or another. The speakers quoted poetry and the Bible and somewhere, down toward the end, they got around to telling us why we should vote for them.

We listened to them politely and to some, even with interest. On the way home, Papa would explain to Mama what they really were saying and tell her which one he thought stood the best chance of winning. I always felt a little sorry for those others who had worked so hard and, in some instances, spoken so beautifully. I thought Papa should have told them (privately, of course) that they didn't have a chance and they might as well stop working so hard at it and spending the money it must take to go running about the country. It seemed a poor way to earn a living—begging people to give you an office.

Never for one moment did I doubt their sincerity. I knew that every one of them meant exactly what he said, and that, if he were elected, he would be honest and good and kind and fair. I wished there was some way that all of them could be elected and then everyone would be happy, including the people in the county.

At least one program would be given over to a "Paper" made up of comments on current affairs, interspersed with jokes gleaned from newspapers and magazines, with the names of people in the community substituted for the original ones. We children suffered the paper for the sake of the jokes.

And once a young man—very clever, one we all knew would go far in the world—read a paper dealing entirely with a trip to the moon. He traveled in a bullet-shaped craft that went swishing through the air at an unbelievable rate of speed. He wore a special suit so that he wouldn't get jolted around, and once on the moon, he saw strange and miraculous things. And we all said, my what an imagination he has. A trip to the moon —think of it!

Toward the end of the season, when it was believed that we children were sufficiently prepared (and, I have since suspected, when the adults were a trifle weary of program planning), an entire evening was given over to such of us as might have pieces learned and were willing to recite. For the most part, these pieces came from our readers or books we had in the school library, and were usually some of the old stand-bys, known to generations of school children.

At such times, we insisted, with more force than understanding, that we preferred death to a curtailment of our liberties; we plucked a flower out of a crannied wall and wondered at it; we ruled that, after four score years and seven we could do nothing more toward establishing the glory of our country at Gettysburg. We agreed life was far from being an empty dream, the quality of mercy was most assuredly not strained, and the barefoot boy had it pretty good.

Not until years later did it occur to me to wonder why the boy stayed on the burning deck to be turned into a crisp rather than getting the you-know-what out of there with the rest of the crew. Although in actual life we might occasionally rebel against parental rulings, we expected our book people to be bigger than life and more noble. The age of debunking had not yet set in. We never doubted that George Washington cut down the cherry tree and responded with proper nobility when questioned; nobody ever so much as hinted that Paul Revere did not finish his famous ride; and we were spared all listings of the frailties of the authors represented in our readers.

We still had heroes and we looked up to them and believed in them. A confidence rooted in ignorance, perhaps, but nevertheless a thing to lean upon until we learned to stand alone.

Moreover, the things we heard and saw and took part in stayed with us. Several years ago I happened to be a guest at a dinner given in New York for Alan Paton, the distinguished South African author. For no reason I can give, he flashed out in the middle of a brisk, bright conversation, the following lines:

> "It was the schooner Hesperus,
> That sailed the wintry sea—"

Automatically, without pausing to take thought, I picked up the cue:

"And the skipper had taken his little daughter,
To bear him company—"

We were off, the two of us, in a joint recitation of "The Wreck of the Hesperus" with the dull throaty roar of New York traffic a background for our words. Educated half a world apart, we still had a common heritage in the poem we had learned in school.

That the Literary Society was, in itself, a heritage to be cherished never occurred to any of us who took part in it. But so it was—local as the schoolhouse, homemade as apple butter, familiar as the friends who took part, and, at the same time, individual as the shape of our noses. Insular, granted, and amateur, undeniably. But for all that, possessing a sturdy naïve originality lacking now in many commercial programs as surely as store bread lacks the flavor of the homemade variety.

A two-way project it was, in which we represented both producer and consumer. And no matter how thin you sliced it, good fun.

XI.

Summer's Sweetness, Stored Away

EVEN if Mama had not said a word to any of us, I think we would have known. Already there was a hint of frost in the air. A thin haze hung over the landscape; "Indian camp-fires," Papa said. Festoons of cobwebs swung from every post and telephone wire. Most of the corn had been put into shocks, or shucked and stored in the barn, leaving the stalks looking like desolation itself. Potbellied pumpkins lay fat and complacent on the ground. And you could not step without scaring up a covey of quail.

So, Mama's casual remark at breakfast, "Don't you think we should make apple butter tomorrow?" brought no real surprise. Mostly we children were pleased if tomorrow happened to be Saturday and we would be free to witness the event.

For an event it truly was, although I cannot put my finger on any single reason for its importance in our lives. It might have been the company that came the evening before to help prepare the apples, or the excitement of the actual ritual, or the samples we snitched, or the promise of good eating to come. Perhaps it was none of these but, rather, the rising of some primitive urge within us which welcomed an incident both ro-mantic and picturesque, one savoring of days long gone and customs only dimly understood.

Running water and electricity and a furnace we might have in the house, and a car to drive and a tractor to pull the farm implements, but when Papa and Mama made apple butter, they went back to the method, detail by detail, which had been followed by their fathers before them, and their grandfathers, and so on far into the past when Missouri highways were yet to be and skins hung on log cabin walls.

Now, as then, neighbors and kin gathered the evening before to help prepare the apples. When we got home from school—where we had been in such a state of anticipation all day that we must have made great nuisances of ourselves—we found everything in readiness for these helpers. Baskets of apples, knives, pans, and the peeler were ready. The kitchen, where the evening's work was to be done, was neat and orderly and smelling delightfully from the still-warm gingerbread intended to serve as refreshments.

There is something inherent in a true Missourian which gives him a feel about apples and their uses. We can toss off their names—Winesaps, Jonathans, Missouri Pippin, York Imperial, Grimes Golden, Delicious, Mammoth Black Twig, Ben Davis—each one meaning to us a distinct and separate flavor, a particular adaptability for certain uses. Without looking now, we knew the baskets would be filled with Winesaps and Jonathans, with Ben Davis filling in only when the others could not be had. And, just as if our lunch boxes had not contained several Winesaps, we now took a couple apiece and ate them, the juice running down our chins. Mama sent us to the bathroom to wash our faces, and said to get cleaned up in a hurry because we were going to eat early, and Sister and I would have to do the dishes, and no dillydallying.

Which was certainly no news to us.

We had scarcely got things cleared away when the help began arriving. Neighbors and several cousins and an uncle and aunt or two, all wearing the self-satisfied look of people who have taken the measure of their task and know they are equal to it. While everybody was glad to see everybody else, and said so, we all knew the chief end was not social, but business. Greetings were exchanged in a hurry, and everybody got down to work.

Papa manned the apple peeler, a small gadget with prongs

for holding the apple in place, a crank to turn by hand, and a rotary knife which ran around the surface of the apple, cutting off the peeling in red spiral-like shavings. When the knife came to the end of its journey, a little gizmo reached out to trip the naked apple into a container provided for the purpose. As simple as that, yet each year it was a miracle to me, fresh, as if I were seeing it for the first time.

As fast as the peeled apples fell into the tub, the workers reached for them, cut each one into perhaps eight sections, discarding core, seeds, and stem. The sound of knives biting through the white juiciness of the fruit mingled with the ceaseless clatter of tongues.

"Many's the time I've heard my grandfather tell about making apple butter during The War." (In Missouri, to this day, we say The War. There have been a few upstart ones since but we give them a name and a number. The Civil War remains, quite simply, The War.) "They looked up and saw a bunch of soldiers coming down the road, so far away nobody could tell which side they were on. Grandpa was all in a sweat, trying to figure out what to do. If he left, the apple butter would burn; if he stayed and faced them, they might be on the other side—"

"They say Myra Field's twins aren't doing a bit well—"

"First time I ever remember seeing apple butter made, I was just a little shaver. A man on a big black horse came riding by, and Pa whispered to me, 'Don't pay him any mind. That's Jesse James—' "

"If you put a little sugar in the pie crust, it browns better—"

The talk shuttled back and forth, from glamorous past to trivial present until Mama stilled busy tongues and hands by bringing out slabs of gingerbread and glasses of sweet cider.

Even this respite did not last long; soon the workers were back at their jobs, to stay with them until the last apple was shorn of its peeling and cut into thin sections, ready for tomorrow's cooking. Then everyone went home, leaving us children to stagger wearily off to bed and Mama and Papa to cover the containers of fruit.

Before it was even light the next morning we children were

awakened by a clanging sound and knew it was Papa taking the apple butter kettle from the granary loft where it was stored between the times of its use. That kettle was the pride of our hearts. Made of copper, it had belonged to our grandfather, Papa's father, and it held more than thirty gallons. Before using it, Mama or the hired girl scoured it with salt and vinegar and washed it afterward with hot water so that its burnished brightness was a joy to see. Sometimes we lent it out, and we children spent an anxious time until it was returned. What if the borrower allowed the contents to burn! What if he should drop it and make a dent! What if the copper should be injured! The generous sample which good taste demanded the borrower bring back as rent was small pay for our day of anxiety. Yet under no circumstances would we have had Papa refuse. The possession of a real copper apple-butter kettle gave prestige in a community, something which could not be overlooked.

We were dressed in no time and outdoors watching Papa as he made the fire back by the woodpile. When he had it to his liking, he called Mama, for now the time had arrived for her advice. She stood by watching, lending both moral support and plenty of suggestions, while he dumped in the apples. There seemed to be an awful lot of them, until we remembered that for every gallon of finished product, there must be two bushels of apples.

"What are you going to do about the liquid?" Papa asked. "What's it to be this time?"

The question was unnecessary, for he knew, well as anything.

"Same as always," Mama said. "Half cider, half water. I never did like all cider—makes it too strong. And all water is wishy-washy."

By now, the fire had died to a steady blaze, well under control. Papa, with the help of the hired man, lifted the full kettle to the iron frame which was to support it over the fire, took the paddle in hand, and the game was on.

At first there was no trick to it at all. Since no sugar had, as yet, been added to the apples, the danger of sticking was small.

Nor had the mixture cooked long enough to "pop," a stage where the stirrer can be spattered with the boiling mixture unless he keeps his wits about him. Before things had got that far, Papa let us have our turn, putting the paddle into our hands for our moment of regency.

We knew all about that paddle. Papa had made it himself when he was scarcely more than a boy. It was fashioned from walnut, the best wood for that purpose. Sycamore is a fair substitute, but pine, fir and cedar must never be used unless you want their own peculiar flavor in your apple butter.

We held the long handle in our hands, now, feeling its dark, polished smoothness, looking down the vista of the years that had brought Papa from a young boy who had made the paddle to the grown man who now presided over our lives. For a moment we had a sense of history, of continuity, of the destiny and purpose of man.

Our turn was short, for soon the contents came to the mushy stage, which meant it was time to add the sugar—a little at a time, with the paddle going vigorously the while. The work took on a new tempo now. Only experienced hands were allowed at the paddle. The hired man, if deemed sharp enough, helped, and any trusty neighbor or relative who might have happened by. The apple butter had begun the critical "popping" stage, sputtering everywhere, landing on the fire with angry hisses. It was midafternoon and from the kitchen came the clinking of glass where Mama and the hired girl, if we had one, and any female friends and relatives in attendance were washing and sterilizing glass jars to receive the apple butter once it was done. In some ways, it was like a birthing, with everyone at a top peak of expectation and excitement.

There was a general concentration of forces around the kettle now. One person was kept busy running back and forth between the woodpile and the fire, putting on wood a little at a time, seeing that the blaze was exactly at the proper degree of heat. Several stood in readiness to spell off the head stirrer (Papa) and all ventured their opinion as to the stage of doneness.

Any Missourian knows there is a just-right stage to apple butter, when, if it is removed from the fire, it will result in a perfect product—thick enough to hold its shape on the plate, smooth as velvet, slightly shiny on top. Less cooking will make it runny; more will make it dry and tasteless. A few times Mama erred on either side and as a result of her failure, remained curiously humble until next fall came, bringing with it a chance for her to redeem herself. Small wonder that now she should be nervously concerned, anxious to try many tests rather than the single one on which Papa pinned his faith.

"They say if you try it on a piece of white paper and it doesn't soak through it's done," she ventured.

"Watch the paddle," Papa told her. "It will tell you—"

"And then there's some who say you can tell by the sound of the 'pop' it makes."

"The paddle—" Papa repeated patiently.

"I have some samples in the kitchen. If the children haven't eaten them—"

Of course we had, with fresh bread and butter. The memory of it was in our mouths, the traces on our faces. Guilt rose up to engulf us. What if our greed had ruined the whole venture?

"There," Papa said triumphantly. "There—see! The path of the paddle has left its print on the surface. It's done."

So Mama grabbed the bag of cinnamon, dumping it into the boiling mass. Just as the last coppery trail disappeared from the surface, two men lifted the kettle from the fire, carrying it to a cooler place. Papa followed, stirring every step of the way, for the contents could still stick and ruin the whole batch. The glass jars were brought out and pretty soon all hands were busy putting apple butter into them.

The excitement was over for another year.

But it would all come back to us some wintry day when snow was spitting against the window panes and a huge fire roared in the kitchen range at our backs and the smell of the grown-ups' coffee filled the air. Mama would pass us the glass bowl then, and we would help ourselves from the garnet-red contents.

Apple butter! Not too sweet, not too sour; smooth as velvet, holding summer's lush promise linked with autumn's rich fulfillment. One taste, and we were back once more in summer, with its delights of taste and smell. It was more than food we ate.

It still comes back to me occasionally on a fine day in autumn with a nostalgia that is not so much regional homesickness as it is a wish to find some fixed and constant thing in a world whose whole order is changed. I comfort myself that, even now, in some parts of Missouri there is a sound of apple-butter kettles being dragged from lofts, of apple peelers whirring, of tongues clattering while busy fingers cut through Winesaps and Jonathans. A smell of woodsmoke, mingled with cider and cinnamon, fills the air while over it all hangs the haze of Indian summer. And someway, I feel that so long as Missourians are still making apple butter, the world can't be in too bad a shape.

XII.

Reading Aloud

HOMEWORK, as such, must be a comparatively recent development in the educational field. Personally, I don't remember hearing much about it during my hitch in grade school. Perhaps we were less well trained than the scholars of today—or maybe we were just smarter and didn't need to spend all day and half the night getting our lessons. It might possibly have been the way a country school was run, with all the students sitting there listening to the others recite. Under that system, you picked up learning by a sort of osmosis. Besides, you could always do your homework while the classes in which you had no interest were reciting.

So, lacking homework, and having neither radio nor TV, it was no wonder we turned to reading aloud on those long winter evenings at home.

The setting for this enterprise was a thing to remember. Apples shining red and juicy cold, just brought up from the cellar. Sometimes a bowl of popcorn seasoned with salt and Mama's home-churned butter. Rarely a plate of fudge or divinity, for candy was sticky and might rub off on the book.

In the early months of fall we had cider taken from the barrel in the cellar. Mama kept a strict eye on the contents seeming to know by instinct the exact moment when it had begun to "turn" and was, therefore, unfit for us to drink. Not until years afterward did I hear of hard cider. All I knew at the time was that cider, so sweet and delicious when first brewed, turned eventually into vinegar which we used in various delicacies such as pickles, both cucumber and peach, relishes, and a yummy mayonnaise we called boiled dressing, concocted from sour cream, whole eggs, appropriate condiments, and, of course, the vinegar.

We also had walnuts. Ours were home-grown, having behind them a charming history, one we children never tired of hearing. It went like this:

When Papa was nine years old, his father indicated the portion of the home farm which was to be his when he grew up and married. Papa's mother, our grandmother, thought it would be a good idea to have a lane of walnut trees leading up the hill to where the house would sit. So she and Papa, equipped with a sharp-pointed stick and a bag of walnuts grown on the home tree, did the planting. At intervals, Papa made an indentation with the stick and dropped a walnut into the resulting hole.

By the time we children came along, the trees had grown, just as Grandmother had planned, and were bearing well. One of my first memories is of that lane of walnut trees. In the fall we harvested the crop, using them throughout the winter in cakes and cookies and candy. And, of course, to eat evenings while we read aloud.

I remember wondering, as a child so often wonders in trying to relate the past to the present, if Papa realized when he planted those seeds so long ago that he would, indeed, build a house on the spot his father set aside for him, and that he would marry Mama (who, we knew, he thought was the most beautiful woman in the world) and bring her home to live in it and that they would have two little girls and a boy who would eat the walnuts from those trees while they sat listening to him read aloud.

Of course, I did not so much as glimpse the extension of the picture—how they would live out the long full years of their married life in that house, never once thinking of moving, adding to it as fancy and a growing family dictated. But even so, it would remain essentially unchanged—strong and sturdy, beautiful and dependable. Like their love for each other, and for us.

Although Papa was the chief reader, Mama occasionally spelled him off, and now and then I, as the oldest, was allowed a turn. I hurried along, trying to get the story. Although I must have butchered some of the words, I remember being stopped only rarely. For goodness sakes, this was for fun, not a device to teach pronunciation.

We read whatever we could lay our hands on. Since we had Dickens in our own library, we were introduced to him early. I wept so loudly at David Copperfield's orphan state that Papa threatened to quit reading if I didn't control myself. (I like to remember, to his everlasting credit, that he did not remind me David was just a little boy in a book, and not a real person.) Thus admonished I got hold of myself, continued to sniff a little, but did not further interrupt the reading. Nobody had so much as hinted that I *ought* to read Dickens, so I finished *David Copperfield* myself, reading ahead of the family, and feeling all smug and set-up because I know what was going to happen even before Papa got to it.

I begged or borrowed all the other books by Dickens I could lay my hand upon, wolfing some down, discarding others I didn't especially care for. Not long ago I heard someone say she tried to read *David Copperfield* and found it too hard, so she stopped.

"I am convinced we start children on these books too young," she said.

Too young, indeed! I think I was in the sixth grade that winter. When critics tell us now that Dickens' star is once more on the ascent, I smile tolerantly. For me, it never went down.

Our tastes were not always of such high caliber. We also read Horatio Alger and thought the moral very good. We read the serials in the *Star* and *Times*, which the rural mail carrier delivered to us daily. I still remember a light adventure piece—I can see the title printed at the top of the page, and the italics giving the synopsis. (I read it, too, just to be sure the late starters weren't missing anything.) I can see the author's name. I can relate a few of the episodes.

Once I did a very sneaky thing. I slipped the paper out and read it as soon as it came. Actually, there was no real reason I shouldn't read the newspaper serial ahead of the others, except for a sort of unwritten understanding among us that we'd wait for the family session. This gentleman's agreement did not extend to books. Those we read when and where we could get our hands on them.

I submit as a record in variety the fact that I read *Pride and Prejudice* and all the Elsie Dinsmore books in one summer. The former we owned; the latter came about in a slightly different way.

The Elsie books were doled out to me by an old lady, a friend of my grandmother's. The series had once belonged to her daughter, now dead. Grandma insisted that I call on her good friend who was very lonely. The first time I went with reluctance, but after that I couldn't get back fast enough, or often enough. She was smart, that old girl was. Each time I went she let me take home with me one of the Elsie books (in sequence). When I returned it, I got another. I don't know how many she actually had, but it was enough to keep me coming back one entire summer. I must admit I skipped the moralizing and read the story line. Nobody can give me many pointers on speed reading. Sometimes I think I started it, just so I could go back for another portion of Elsie's adventures.

Pride and Prejudice I took more slowly. After all, it was on hand and I didn't have to return it. As a result, I can't begin to say how many times I reread it. Not so often as I did *John Halifax,* however, which I reread once every summer, regularly. On my first trip to England, I spent six weeks in the home of my British publisher and his wife. They marveled that I fitted in so well. "Almost like a real Britisher," they said.

"In a way I grew up here," I assured them.

And I had. Those long evenings when Papa read Dickens to

us, or Jane Austen or Stevenson or Dinah Maria Mulock—those summer afternoons when I read them for myself—had prepared me for this land so that I felt a sense of homecoming.

The summer I read Jane Austen I also discovered Zane Grey's westerns, which a friend loaned to me. By this time Sister was big enough to join me, and we sat cross-legged under a big maple, reading Zane Grey together. We skimmed along, skipping portions we found dull. She insists that in one afternoon we read three books, passing them from hand to hand as we finished. I can't give statistics, but I do know we gulped those books down.

Admittedly, my reading background is spotty. If book clubs existed, we knew nothing about them. If there was such a thing as a required reading list for students, with points attached to each book title like items priced in a supermarket, it had escaped our teacher's notice. Or, having seen it, she wisely ignored it. We lived and died by the *Kansas City Star* and *Times*, believing every word we read therein, somehow feeling that the great earthly reward for a long and virtuous and self-sacrificing life was a four-line obit on the back page of that paper. The *Star* had, I believe, a book page on Saturday evening, but I don't ever remember paying it any mind. For goodness sakes, books were to be read, not to read about. Besides, we weren't going to let anybody tell us what to read or what to think about it, once we read it. That was a personal matter, individual as falling in love and getting religion.

Anyway, you read what you had on hand, supplemented by such volumes as you could get from the school library or borrow from friends. And what we had on hand at our house was a mixture. Emerson's *Representative Men* (Papa's own book) and Porter's *Pollyanna* (which ran in the *Star*). Sir Walter Scott and *Daddy Long-Legs*. *The Wide, Wide World* and *Scottish Chiefs*. *Little Lord Fauntleroy* (from the school library) and *Tom Sawyer* (which someone gave me for Christmas). We read *Tom Sawyer* aloud the same winter we read a smugly moralizing book called *The Widow O'Callagan's Boys* and I thought the former was much the better of the two.

Of course, every child growing up in our part of Missouri read *Order Number Eleven,* the novel about the infamous order of that name given by Colonel Ewing during The War, ordering three counties of western Missouri to be depopulated as a retaliation for Quantrill's raid on Lawrence, Kansas. We were also familiar with Caleb Bingham's picture bearing the same name, depicting the plight of the families so displaced. The story of Order Number Eleven and the misery resulting from it was a legend handed down to us by our grandparents on both sides of the house.

Only a few years ago, when I was doing research for a book dealing in part with that portion of our history, I ran across the information that Bingham had made it his business to distribute his picture dramatizing the unnecessary devastation brought about by Ewing's order. This picture played a part in defeating Ewing when he ran for governor of Ohio, a position which would have made him a natural for possible nomination as Vice-President or even President of the United States.

Another interesting side light on Order Number Eleven had even more important repercussions. Some of Lincoln's enemies in the East chose to interpret the horrors resulting from Ewing's order, together with the Lawrence raid which brought it about, as proof that the President was neglecting the protection of the western border. Because of this, they attempted to block his nomination for a second term.

Lincoln's nomination was made sure, so the story goes, by the moving speech of Jim Lane, Senator from Kansas, whose suicide later resulted in the appointment of Edmund G. Ross. It was Ross's single vote which is commonly given credit for saving President Johnson from conviction at the impeachment trial.

Not only did we read aloud at home, we also practiced this skill at school. When our turn came, we stood up and read whatever portion was assigned to us. I remember becoming so carried away with myself when it came my turn to read the casket scene from *The Merchant of Venice* that I took the class, and apparently the teacher, along with me to such good effect that I wasn't stopped at the logical place and made to yield my honor to another. Instead, I finished with a great flourish, and when I sat down, I was applauded. Heady brew, that.

We read portions from Mallory's Arthurian legends, *The King of the Golden River*, *The Courtship of Miles Standish*, *Evangeline*, *Hiawatha*, *The Legend of Sleepy Hollow* and much of Hawthorne.

We also were exposed to the sparse, diamond-clear prose of the Greek legends; Ulysses and Telemachus and Jason and the rest of them were as well known as were the characters in the lightest, most inconsequential book we read.

And we did read those inconsequential ones.

Once a hired girl let me borrow one of her books. Instinctively I knew, perhaps by the furtive manner in which the loan was made, that this wasn't to be read aloud, nor even to share with Sister. I went upstairs to my room, flung myself, stomach down, on the bed, and began to gulp the book. I have no notion how long I had been reading when I looked up and saw Papa standing beside me. What had brought him upstairs I will never know. Probably Mama had told him to go find me and set me to some task (for he was not one to snoop).

I sat upright with a jerk, trying, at the same time, to hide the book. It was too late! Papa had already seen it.

"You know," he remarked casually, "I wouldn't read that if I were you. It's nothing but trash."

Then I saw the book for what I had known it to be all along —not pornography or smut or violence or anything like that, although, I am sure, all were implied. It was trash—just pure, unmitigated trash. I gave it back to the hired girl, not even bothering to answer when she asked me how I liked it. To this day the one thing I cannot forgive in a book is trashiness.

Although we read the Bible—Papa himself possessed a most thorough knowledge of the Book—it was not our custom to have Scripture reading and prayer except on special occasions, a practice I still think made the experience all the more impressive. Naturally when a minister came calling, Papa handed him the family Bible, with its record of his and Mama's marriage and the dates of our births. There were flowers and delicate scrolls on these pages, an altogether lovely sight. The minister would read and afterward pray while we all felt the deep solemnity of the occasion. It was almost like being in church. One time, however, things didn't turn out so well.

A new minister came, very young and unsure, but all the more intense for that very reason. To complicate matters, we allowed the little dog Fleas to stay in the room during the Bible reading and prayer, a great mistake on our part. This we realized the moment the young man began, but we didn't dare interrupt him, so ill-at-ease he was, and embarrassed, and all. We sat still, hoping for the best.

It was a hope without foundation.

Fleas behaved well enough during the reading, cocking his little black head to one side, listening intently as a child. The minister finished, closed the book. "Let us pray," he said, and knelt beside his chair.

We slid on our knees, being accustomed to doing so at such times. To Fleas, however, it was a new experience. He regarded us curiously. He came to sniff the soles of my feet. Then, apparently deciding this must be some sort of a new game in which he was supposed to do his part, he gave a joyful yip and went to the chair where Brother knelt. Before Brother or Papa or anyone could reach out to stop him, he dashed to Sister, and then, still yipping at the top of his lungs, to Mama. Papa stood up, red-faced, and far from being in a prayerful mood. He laid firm hands on the little dog. The minister, stopped in the middle of a sentence, looked up uncertainly, as if he had not quite decided whether to forego praying for this unpredictable family, or to intervene with even more fervor.

Papa had Fleas by the scruff of the neck now. As he walked toward the door, he turned to say, "We pray, of course. But the little dog has not seen us kneel before."

The young minister got to his feet. "I understand," he said. But he didn't sound too convincing.

Papa put the dog outside and came back. By this time, Mama

and we three children were on our feet, and it was only because Mama gave us a Look that we were restraining our laughter.

"Go ahead," Papa said to the minister. "Be good enough to finish the prayer."

The young man gulped a couple of times, probably thinking we were beyond help, and then decided to go on. He finished the prayer, but it was a mighty short one. And this time we stood up.

We learned Bible verses to say at Sunday school. Sometimes we learned them by rote, not knowing the meaning, but still saying the words. Or, as was the case of a small cousin, saying what we believed them to be.

"What was your Bible verse today?" her mother asked.

"Learn to fry meat," she flashed back, quick as a wink.

It took her mama a rather longish time to figure out what she really had learned was, "Learn to be meek."

The magnificent prose of the Bible, however, is like great music. One does not need to understand it all in order to have it place its mark on you.

Poetry is, of course, one of the best things of all to read aloud. I remember well a set of ten volumes, rather small in size, red in color, which we got with a subscription to some magazine. We were at the dinner table the day the rural mail carrier delivered them (of course it was midday) and somebody —Brother, probably—went out to get the mail. We cut the string impatiently and there they were, those ten lovely books.

By this time Bill was living with us. A double first cousin (his mother had been my father's sister; his father, my mother's brother) he came to us after his mother's death, when he was still quite young. It was like having another brother in the family. Of course, he shared our love of reading.

We divided the volumes among the six of us and, the meal neglected, began to thumb through them.

"Here," someone would say. "Here's a good one—"

We listened, especially since we had our own choice bit we wanted to read in turn.

"Here's a good one," Bill said.

He read from Kipling:

> "He must go—go—go—away from here!
> On the other side of the world he's overdue."

And then, from a lesser poet:

> "Out there somewhere along the sea a ship is waiting
> patiently,
> While up the beach the bubbles slip with white
> afloat between."

We all thought it sounded wonderfully romantic and free and yearned to be off somewhere to strange and distant places.

Then the time came when there was a ship waiting to take Bill, literally, to the other side of the world. He tells the story of how one night, in the Pacific theater of war, with the enemy snipers around him and things pretty rough and wholly unromantic, he read poetry by a flashlight, hidden under his blanket. And thus he was taken back, briefly, to home and reading aloud.

Well he might have been, for it was, indeed, an experience to remember. I wonder—do families ever read aloud any more?

Winter

XIII.

"The Least of These——"

HAD there been such a thing as an Establishment mentioned in my young days, or a brand of earthly hierarchy, I could have rattled off the order of importance of its members without even stopping for breath. First, of course, was Papa who was the smartest, bravest, finest man in the world. Next would be a dual listing—the current Presiding Elder and Dr. Carney. I must confess I included the church dignitary only because I thought it was proper to do so. He was almost a legendary character who came only at the time of Quarterly Meeting, was listened to with awe and fed fried chicken until it was a wonder he could so much as open his mouth, much less give his sermon.

Dr. Carney was a different case entirely. We knew and loved him in person, year in, year out. He had brought my mother into the world and all of her brothers and sisters as well. In time he was to preside at the entrances of us three children, as well as those of various cousins scattered over the countryside. If he came and looked at us and said there was nothing much the matter, we got well and no nonsense about it in spite of how sick we had thought we were before he arrived. That was why, the winter the flu hit our community, Aunt Lil did what he told her to, even though she was scared to death to carry out his orders.

It happened like this!

We had one Needy Family in our town, a shiftless lot, with

innumerable children and no visible means of support. Mr.
Belden, the father, worked now and then when it suited him,
but he wasn't much good at anything. Mrs. Belden took in
washing, but the kids were always crawling around over the
clothes, making a great mess of them, so nobody would send
her anything really particular. The oldest boy was big enough
to work, but if you set him to mowing the lawn he'd like as
not cut off a toe with the grass hook, or step on a stick which
would fly up and come close to braining him, so most people
didn't want him around. Somehow, though, the Beldens managed to keep a roof over their heads and eat, after their fashion.
And naturally, since they represented our Needy Family, we
looked after them.

The first Christmas after they came to town, Mama decided
to fix them a Christmas basket.

"Poor things," she said, "they won't have much, I'm afraid.
We must help them."

Seeing that we were quite overwhelmed by the Belden's sad
state, Mama decided to drive the lesson home even more force-
fully.

"Remember," she told us, "Inasmuch as you have done it unto
the least of these—"

We finished the Bible verse from memory, running errands
like mad in order that we might be in on such a noble endeavor.

Mama had Papa kill one of the fattest hens which she dressed,
wings akimbo and legs trussed up nicely with a separate package
made of liver and gizzard. She wrapped it all in waxed paper and
put it into a basket, together with several cans of fruit and
vegetables and glasses of jelly, all harvested from summer's
plenty. Papa brought potatoes and turnips from the cellar and
we were set to scrubbing them. Brother suggested the addition
of apples and some ears of popcorn. When it was all assembled,
the basket had truly gigantic proportions. So we all dressed up
—not in our best, for we did not wish to embarrass the Beldens
—to deliver the gift in person, since that was the approved
method of gift-bearing.

We went to the door, Papa carrying the basket, staggering under its weight. Mama knocked and a languid voice bade her "Come in." We hesitated a moment, but since nobody bothered to open the door, we turned the knob and went in.

Mr. Belden lay sprawled out on a beat-up old couch, one foot trailing off the edge. Mrs. Belden was shuffling a very dirty deck of cards. Assorted children ranged around the room, regarding us with unblinking stares and fingers-in-mouths.

"Oh, how-de-do," Mrs. Belden cried cheerfully. "I was just fixin' to tell Mr. Belden's fortune."

"I thought we'd bring you a little Christmas gift," Mama said, looking around her uncertainly. And, since she had no help at all from the mistress of the house, Mama signaled Papa to put the basket on the table. He did so, pushing aside the dirty dishes in order to make room.

Mrs. Belden stood up. Dirty she was, and almost ragged, but still there was a certain dignity about her.

"We thank you," she said. "That's the first we've got."

It is a wonder we did not burst with an excess of virtue right there on the spot. Just to think of it—no one else had thought of these poor people in our midst. We told her, with all the modesty we could muster, that it was nothing at all and we hoped they enjoyed it and had a Merry Christmas. This done, we all backed out and made our way to Aunt Lil's, there to do a little discreet bragging.

Our story, instead of bringing words of praise, got only a great gale of laughter from our town aunt.

"There's been a constant stream of people going there all day long, taking them food and gifts and even coal," she said. "And do you know what she's told every one of them?"

We said no, but we looked at each other a little weakly. We could guess.

"She's said to each one '*Thank you, that's the first we've got!*'"

"Well," Mama began uncertainly. Then continued, sounding almost defiant, "I'm still glad we took the basket."

"Of course," Aunt Lil agreed. "You couldn't have enjoyed your own Christmas if you hadn't done something for them."

"But to accept the gift and never let on anyone else had been there." Mama couldn't be quite sure, even now, that she wasn't a little hot under the collar about the whole business.

"Now look here," Aunt Lil told her, "how would you have felt if she had said, 'That's real nice of you, but we already have more than we need.'?"

We had to admit, albeit reluctantly, that maybe after all Mrs. Belden chose the kinder way.

"At that you were lucky," Aunt Lil went on. "Mrs. Garner took a turkey and dressing and goodness knows what all. And Mr. Belden just peered at the basket while Mrs. B. was giving that old first-we've-got-line and asked, 'But whar be the cranberry sarse?' "

"He takes it for granted," Mama said. "I've a good mind to go back and pick up my basket. Or maybe Mrs. Garner's turkey."

We all laughed at the idea of Mama's stealing the turkey and then we went on to talk of other things.

The Beldens had, indeed, taken their multitude of gifts for granted and probably never felt in the least degree that they were receiving charity. Nor, in all likelihood, did it occur to us. We delivered the gifts in person instead of turning them over to an agency, which in turn doled out what seemed best suited to the occasion. We did not give a check in order to have a record for income tax purposes. We saw the Beldens as our individual responsibility and acted accordingly. Of course, this haphazard method resulted in duplication and waste, but at the same time we got a fine glow that lasted well into the new year.

Feeling our responsibilities as we did, it was no wonder Aunt Lil did what Dr. Carney told her to when he came to her door one morning, early, driven by the colored man who looked after him as if he were a child, although by now he was getting along in years. Waving aside the cup of coffee she urged upon him, he got immediately into the business of the hour.

"Lillie," he said, "Mrs. Belden is getting ready to have another baby and she has the flu."

"Oh, my goodness," Aunt Lil said.

That dread word was just beginning to make itself felt in our community. The *Star* and *Times* had accounts—the widespread nature of the epidemic, the grave dangers. "Flu, oh my goodness, our first case."

"Get ready," Dr. Carney said. "You're going with me."

"Not me," she told him flatly.

"Yes, you. I'll put a mask over your face so you can't breathe the germs. I need a woman to help me, and you're going."

She went.

Mr. Belden took the covey of Belden children off somewhere for the duration, and Dr. Carney and Aunt Lil (wearing her mask which, she said later, flapped up and down like a sheet in a high wind—she was that scared and breathed so hard and fast) got the baby into the world. Poor little thing—it never even breathed. Aunt Lil called Mama, and together they prepared the small body for burial (Mama, too, wearing a mask), using some baby clothes Mama had left over from the three of us. When they had finished, they took the infant in for Mrs. Belden and Mr. Belden, now returned from his enforced absence, to see. Mrs. Belden touched the little hand weakly and two tears rolled down her cheeks.

Mr. Belden reached out to rearrange a small cuff on the dress, which was a bit on the crooked side.

"There's a right and a wrong way to do everything," he said. "Now, it looks better."

We buried the Belden baby, decently and with dignity, in a graveside service. The preacher said a few words and gave a prayer, and someone sang a song about Jesus loving the little children. There were some flowers—Mrs. Mauldin donated a potted begonia. And nobody said that hateful word, charity, either then or afterward. For goodness sakes, the Beldens were our neighbors, when you got right down to it, and they were in trouble, and at times like that you looked after your own.

Certainly hired girls were not to be lumped in with the likes of the Beldens, but even so we felt a certain responsibility for them and a wish to preserve their dignity and self-respect. Sometimes they would be distant kin or kin to kin. I can remember visiting young friends of mine and being introduced to the woman or girl busy about the kitchen and having her identified as "Cousin Lura." Then the information would be added, "She's helping us this summer."

Seldom, if ever, did we call them hired girls.

Or maybe it was an older woman, lonely, indigent, with no place to go. (Now, of course, she could enter a Sunset Years Co-operative.) It might be a young girl from a big family, desperately in need of money. Or maybe a sister-in-law's cousin, twice removed. You probably would have sent them money in any event, but this way they could save their pride and help a little, and things worked out better all around.

Once Mama was called upon to render service of another nature in this matter of hired girls. She agreed to take Goldie Givens into her home, look after her, and pay her a little something a week. She had only one relative, a cousin named Bessie, who lived by herself in a small, drab house just at the edge of town. Whenever Mama and her sisters got around to mentioning Bessie's name, they lowered their voices and exchanged knowing looks.

Of course Mama saw her duty clearly and agreed to take Goldie, especially since her Cousin Bessie didn't want her.

Goldie was a thorn in Mama's side. She had no knowledge of how to cook, keep house, wash dishes, make beds, or do any other useful thing; nor, as a matter of fact, had she any wish to learn. Mama bore this with all the patience she could muster, reminding herself the poor girl had never had a chance. But one night this patience broke when Goldie went off with the neighbor's hired man in a borrowed buggy and didn't come home until midnight. Even then, they sat out in front quite a while.

Mama, wearing a wrapper over her nightgown, met Goldie at the door and the lid blew off. (The raised voices woke us up, and we came downstairs thinking maybe to find somebody sick or the house on fire.)

"Do you know what time it is?" Mama asked in a tone which, some years later, came to be very familiar to me.

Mama went on to give Goldie a Good Talking To, which, of course, Goldie wasn't about to take without answering back.

"You're not going to stay in my house and come home this hour of the night," Mama told her.

"Who says so?" Goldie asked impudently.

"I say so. You're not quite sixteen and under my care."

Without answering, Goldie started across the room, on the run. When she got to the phone, she took down the receiver and began whirling the crank.

"What are you going to do?" Mama asked.

"I'm going to call Cousin Bessie to come get me."

"At this hour?"

"She won't be in bed yet."

"I doubt that," Mama said crisply. (It was a long time before the full significance of this remark came through to me.) "Even so, though, you're not going to call her. What would Central think!"

"You can't stop me." Goldie's voice rose in a sharp crescendo. "I hate you—so high and mighty and uppity—"

She gave the crank the start of a turn.

"Stop that," Mama said. Never had I seen Mama move so fast as she did then, not even the time the mean old cow took out after Brother.

"You're not going to stop me," Goldie wailed.

"Oh, yes I am."

"How—?"

Mama put her hand on the phone, ran it across the top and then down to the receiver hook.

"By disconnecting the phone," she said calmly. "Now, you go to bed and get some sleep."

For one long moment Goldie sat there, making no move to

obey. Suddenly all fight seemed to go out of her, and she was only a scared young girl. She got up meekly.

"Yes, ma'am," she said. And went off to bed.

The funny thing is I don't remember the next morning at all, nor very much of the weeks that followed. Goldie stayed on, and it seems to me she was a little better about helping. I do know she treated Mama with a new respect. When she left in the fall, we were sorry to see her go.

To this day, I wonder if she really believed Mama could disconnect the phone, short of cutting the wire with a pair of scissors. Each year we had Christmas cards from Goldie and finally the word that she had married.

"He's a good honest man," she said. "Owns his own business."

That had a fine sound, owning his own business. She didn't say what it was, but no matter. A man with get-up-and-go enough to start out for himself was bound to have something to him.

That's the way we felt about Albert Allerdyne, the peddler, who came twice a year, walking down the country road, his pack on his back. Nobody really thought much of his merchandise—except, of course, the children—declaring it sleazy and second-rate. Still, the women in the community greeted him cordially enough, asked about his health, and offered him a cup of coffee or lemonade, depending on the season. If he happened in at mealtime, he got invited, as a matter of course, to share the food. Nobody called the Better Business Bureau to check his credentials, and above all, nobody had a sign over the door saying "No agents, peddlers, or solicitors admitted here."

Everyone accepted him for what he was—a man trying to make an honest living in the one way he knew.

There was an established ritual accompanying the visit. He always came to the side door and, once admitted, made his way to the kitchen, since the heavy pack could do no injury to the' linoleum. Easing the pack off his back, he seated himself on the chair Mama offered him. Albert said Mama looked well and inquired after Papa. He said the children were certainly growing and the coffee Mama made was better, if anything, than usual.

Often, there was a slice of cake or some cookies to go with it, and he told her they excelled anything she had previously offered him.

He ate with fastidious care, his lean dark face reflecting grave pleasure. It was more than food—he was paying a social call and recognized the importance of the occasion. He was no longer a strange little alien, but a friend breaking bread with friends.

The eating finished, he wiped his hands carefully on the napkin.

"Now," he said, in a speech pattern impossible to imitate, although I am sure I would recognize it if I should hear the first syllable in the dark, somewhere on the surface of the moon, "Now—we will look!"

He brought his merchandise out: lengths of material neatly folded. Tablecloths, laces, linens. Shoestrings and combs and notions of various kinds.

"Ver-ee good . . ." he would insist, lifting each one, looking in Mama's face for encouragement, then placing the article in the lid of his case. "Ver-ee ver-ee pretty. So? Not like the stuff in stores."

"Very pretty," Mama agreed. "Nothing like the things in the stores."

She always bought something, and then the real fun began. Once Mama had counted out the sum of the purchase, Albert rummaged into a part of his pack, as yet unopened, and came out with some trinket for each of us children. Beads or maybe a ribbon for Sister and me. A slingshot for Brother. Things of no real value but yet beyond estimate of worth. For these were the visible recognition that he, too, had something to give, and that, for a while, he was friend and guest in our home.

We thanked him nicely and he said, "You like, yes?" and repacked his bag and told us good-by and left. Mama followed him to the door, wishing him well and he walked off, out into the road. It always seemed to me he held his shoulders a little straighter as he went away.

"Well," Mama said after he was gone, "that really isn't much of a tablecloth I bought from him, but I do declare, I don't know how to say no to him."

Even I could see the cloth was shoddy. Still, I was glad Mama hadn't turned him away.

"I guess I do it because I feel a little better myself when I buy.'"

That was the pre-motel age. When you traveled, you stayed with relatives, no matter how distant, or with friends or friends of friends or kin to kin. In looking back, I seem to remember a constant stream of them all summer long, although my estimate might be colored by the fact that I had to do extra dishes.

Not always did we receive advance warning; the guests sometimes drove up unannounced, apparently confident of welcome. No matter what you were doing, you were supposed to be cordial and gracious and provide free bed and board until such time as they decided to move on. Mercifully, this was usually after a day or two, but now and then a group decided to use our place as a vacation spot and stayed for a real visit. After all, I guess they liked the looks of the place, with its tennis court and croquet ground and pond for fishing and catalpa grove for picnics; with the smokehouse full of hams and bacon, a chicken yard teeming with fryers, a garden thick with every kind of vegetable native to our soil, and an orchard laden with fruit. To say nothing of a cellar loaded down with jams, jellies, and suchlike.

I don't remember ever hearing Mama protest, but I was cast in a lesser mold. I recall standing at a pan full of dirty dishes after a carload of somebody's in-laws had just driven away after a three-day visit without even offering to help carry the dishes to the kitchen. This had been an unusually trying bunch—picky about their food, selfish with the bathroom, and noisy all over the place. I could tell even Mama was glad to be rid of them. When she came back to the kitchen, after having sped the parting guests, she was sharp with me.

"Now get busy on those dishes," she said. "We have a lot to do. You know the Blakelys are coming this evening."

Of course I knew it. The mail carrier had left the card in our box this noon. The Blakelys were on their way to Colorado and were going to stop off if it would be all right with us. It had been years since they had seen us.

Years, indeed! We met them when we visited a cousin once upon a long ago, and since then had exchanged Christmas cards. That was the extent of our friendship.

"I'm getting good and sick of all this company," I snapped. "Our place is like Methodist Communion Sunday—as these quietly go, let others take their places."

Mama looked at me, too horrified to speak. I had committed two cardinal sins—blasphemy and inhospitality. I didn't know how she planned to punish me—I couldn't hope to be sent to bed, with all these dirty dishes in the sink. Suddenly Mama began to laugh.

"It wouldn't be so bad if they'd only go quietly," she said.

So, I was forgiven. I don't know when I ever felt closer to Mama than I did that blessed minute, standing there by the side of a pan full of dirty dishes, laughing together.

Mama decided to go the whole way. "I must admit I'm a little tired of all this extra company," she confessed, her candor endearing her even more to me. "But—that's a part of life, and we have to take it the way it comes."

Indeed it was a part of life as we lived it, and above the inconvenience we knew in entertaining people who were often only the merest acquaintances, I think we felt a sense of reward and even pleasure. We put our hearts into the things we did for others, and in so doing, discovered along with Sir Launfal that the gift without the giver was bare.

There are times now when I suspect the giver is the one who has lost out somewhere down the road. Then, we knew personally the recipients of our bounty and were able to rejoice with them. Now we give an impersonal sum of money and never know who actually gets the benefits from it.

At no time did we feel this sense of personal responsibility more than in winter time, when not only the needy and the stranger within our gates might require succor, but the animal and fowl, and yes, the plant, world as well. Sitting in the house on a bitter winter night, listening to the sleet slither against the window pane, we had a double sense of security and well-being. For not only were we ourselves secure, with a bin full of coal and a cellar full of food, but, likewise, all the lives for which we were responsible were taken care of, down to the barn cats who were doubtless now burrowed deep in the hay loft, dining on mice, which should be caught.

Like Noah, we were cherishing life that, come spring, would replenish the earth. It's a wonder we didn't get a God complex and become impossible to live with.

XIV.

They Took the Children with Them

IN some respects, winter was the most delightful season of
the year, for then we consolidated our gains, taking a rest
from the demands of the other three seasons and catching up
with ourselves. Especially was it a time for parties and for what
we called in our neighborhood "sitting 'til bedtime," a quaint
phrase I have never heard elsewhere and which most certainly
had been carried over from an earlier era, for our part of the
country went back far into the history of the state.

Now people say casually, "Why don't you run by?" That's
what "sitting 'til bedtime" was. Of course, you called first, to
see that it suited, which gave the whole arrangement an air of
excitement and purpose. And, equally of course, it was a family
enterprise. That is why, I suppose, I remember so well the one
time which departed from the familiar custom.

Several of Mama's younger brothers and sisters, together with
some of their friends, were spending the week end with us. Since
the night was brisk and clear, with a full moon, the young
visitors decided it would be fun to walk to see the family who
lived only a short distance away. Accordingly, the customary
phone call was made, and the neighbors said it would be fine—
come right on.

Sister and I scurried away to wash our faces and change our
clothes before Mama had to remind us. As it happened, she put

a stop to this excess of virtue before we so much as started. She said we weren't going.

"Why?" Our wails filled the house.

I don't remember the exact reason. It may have been because Mama considered us too young for a night call—that was before Brother's birth, so we were of tender years. Maybe she thought one of us had the sniffles, which was probably true. Maybe she just wanted the young visitors to have an evening unencumbered with us children. Whatever it was, her ruling held. Papa was to stay at home with us, and that settled the matter. Our yowls were stopped by Papa's wink, meaningful yet sly. Mama should have been suspicious of our quick capitulation, but apparently she wasn't.

"Be good girls," she said. "You'll be asleep by the time I get home, but I'll see you in the morning."

No sooner was she out of the house, than Papa, who didn't like being left either, set things in motion. We began a frantic search about the house for mittens, overshoes, and caps while he went to saddle Nell and bring her to the back gate. Sister and I scuttled out to meet him and he pulled us up by the simple expedient of having us put a small foot on his as it rested in the stirrup. Sister sat in front, cradled in his arms, and I behind with my own arms tight about his waist.

When he was sure we were secure and in place, he started off, cutting across the field catty-wampus, knowing that, if we managed right, we would arrive ahead of the others who were walking the road which made a right angle. I can still remember the brightness of the moon shining in the cold, winter-blue sky, the rush of wind past my small face, the sound of Nell's hoofs on the ground. I also remember the look on Mama's face when she walked in to find Papa and Sister and me sitting demurely in our chairs, having arrived ahead, just as Papa planned it. And the way the neighbor laughed at the joke we had played on the others.

I do not recall that Mama was put out with us. A bit disgusted, perhaps, because Papa had not taken time to make us change our dresses. Everyone settled down for a good evening, with the elders playing Rook in the living room and the children playing dominoes in the kitchen. And all of us eating popcorn and apples and, later, pie and cookies, with coffee for the grownups and hot chocolate for us children. At a suitable hour we set off for home, the young visitors walking, Mama riding sideways on Papa's saddle with Sister in her lap, and me behind her. Papa walked along beside us.

Once Mama, balanced precariously as she was, put her hand on Papa's shoulder to steady herself. His own hand went up to cover hers. Such a simple gesture, almost reflexive in nature. Yet, young as I was, I could sense a moment of tenderness between Mama and Papa which, in some magic way, reached out to include Sister and me as well.

I don't believe they even mentioned our unexpected appearance at the party. True, it had been a bit spectacular (and actually, a case of downright disobedience to orders), but still the principle was sound. For we belonged to a period and to a society in which members took their children with them practically everywhere they went. We were light years away from the era of the baby sitter.

That was the age of Sunday visiting, of second table dinners, of asking everyone you knew or happened to see to go home with you. No cook counted the chops in order to be sure she had enough to go around and then maybe one or two left over so that the plate wouldn't look lonesome after everyone was served. Just before the meal was ready, someone was sent to take a count of the number—usually an adolescent girl, consciously important. She couldn't ever be completely accurate, especially at these wintertime meals, for people kept shifting from room to room. It was like trying to get little chickens into a coop. Finally she had made a fairly close check, however, and the adults were herded into the dining room to eat at the first table.

Brother maintains that, under this system, he was a good fourteen years old before he knew chickens had anything but drumsticks. Even so, no self-respecting child would have chosen to eat at the table with the grownups. Not only did he prefer the companionship of his peers, but he also liked the lack of supervision of table manners either in the kitchen or on the porch or, which was considerably less fun, at the main table after the adults had finished. They always took such an unconscionable time to eat.

After dinner, everyone scattered—the men together, the women to wash the dishes and then gather into their own tight-knit circle, the children to the yard in summer and an upstairs bedroom in winter.

Wherever we went, we were pretty much on our own, left to handle everything save real emergencies. We worked out our own system of rules and checks and balances. I think I was five when I learned the code.

I was the strange child at the Sunday dinner—all the others were either kin to one another or close friends. A new experience for me, usually knee deep in relatives. To make the occasion even more unusual, we were having one of those deceptively warm winter days—a real weather breeder, the old-timers called it. The children decided to go outside and play. I'm sure we were encouraged in this activity by the hostess herself, who must have feared for her furnishings, since children, like young mule colts, are especially wild just before a change in weather.

We made a circle to play drop the handkerchief, and nobody, *nobody* dropped it behind me.

"You're mean," I finally wailed. "I'm company and nobody is nice to me. I'm going to tell Mama."

I started off to carry out my threat when behind me rose the derisive taunt:

"Tattletale, tattletale! Tell Mama without fail!"

I stopped dead in my tracks, an idea struggling to get into my small brain. Maybe you didn't tell Mama, even though you were only five and everybody was mean to you. I turned uncertainly; slowly, tentatively, I made my way back to the circle. The two children I had been standing between, before I flounced away, broke hands matter-of-factly. Timidly I put my little paws back into their hands. The circle closed again, without comment. For a while nothing happened, but I didn't really expect it to. Then there was a flutter of white behind me. I grabbed the handkerchief and shot around the ring, happier than I had been the whole day of the visit. I had been incorporated into the group; what was more, I had earned my membership.

I never mentioned the matter to Mama, and I feel sure no other child felt the necessity of telling her mama. This was a thing to handle for one's self. Of course, had the matter been really important, like a broken arm or a bad stomach-ache, I would have gone howling for help, made confident by the knowledge it was no farther away than the living room. Even in minor difficulties, it was comforting to know our parents were close at hand, a substantial realness in the background. Like money in the bank saved for a rainy day, its very presence seemed to ward off the rain.

There was another side to the coin. Not only did the presence of our parents help us but I think they gained something from having us around as well. For instance, there was the case of Mr. Higgins and the new teacher.

The occasion was a Christmas party at somebody's house, with innumerable rooms and wide staircases where the boys and girls of courting age liked to sit, two by two, and a piano in the front living room where any number of people could gather around and sing, and a back living room where the more staid ones could sit and talk, and even a sort of sun porch where anyone so minded could go to play dominoes and Rook. Oh, it was a very proper house in which to have a party, with the Christmas tree at the front window adding to the general air of festivity.

The new schoolteacher had arrived only a couple of weeks before, fresh out of college, replacing poor Miss Minnie Perkins whose mother was gravely ill. The newcomer was young and very pretty and—let's face it—a bit on the wild side, having come from Kansas City, which had different ways from ours. Mr. Higgins took one look at her and began to make a great fool out of himself.

Actually it was nothing more than a rather conspicuous flirtation on Mr. Higgins' part, very like the antics of a junior high school boy when a new girl enrolled in school. And, it must be confessed, the new teacher acted the part of the new girl, preening herself and entering into the game. Poor Mrs. Higgins, humiliated and sick at heart, did not regard the matter so lightly. Nor did her neighbors and friends—to say nothing of a goodly sprinkle of relatives—who were witness to the episode. The matter was even more grave because Mr. Higgins' flock was watching their father making a complete idiot out of himself.

The women at the party rallied round, much as horses are said to do when the group threatened by Siberian wolves—heads together, heels out, ready for defense. The men watched this gathering with both unease and foreknowledge, realizing their own part in the matter. They were supposed to add their weight of disapproval, snubbing Mr. Higgins, but, if necessary, to go over, clap him on the back and say, "See here, Higgins old boy, how about a game of dominoes?"

I was only eleven, but even so, I was well aware of what was going on. It was not Mrs. Higgins alone to whom the group rallied, but the whole structure of home and family and community solidarity as well. Anything that threatened these institutions, even though it was nothing more than a harmless flirtation, was a group concern. They knew, with an instinct sure as time itself, that the dignity and sanctity of marriage was no light thing, for if it went to pieces, society itself was beginning to crumble. So they marshaled their forces, much as the people of Holland rush to mend even the most insignificant leak in the dikes.

Of course, nobody was that articulate about the matter, not even in their minds. They just said Mr. Higgins was making a fool of himself, and this shouldn't happen with the children watching. And, since the children usually were in evidence at almost any party the members of the community attended, Mr. Higgins finally left the teacher alone. Partly this may have been due to a wish to reinstate himself in the eyes of his peers, partly he couldn't keep on with his children underfoot, or, most likely of all, the young unattached men of the community took over and began courting the new teacher.

At any rate, things worked out, and Mr. Higgins came back into the fold. The women reserved judgment, watching him for some time, until finally the whole episode was forgotten or, at least, crowded into the background. We probably had a lot of activities coming up, such as the oyster supper and Christmas and the Literary Society and Sunday dinners and plenty of parties. Everybody was so busy, we just didn't have time to think about Mr. Higgins, who was, after all, behaving like a model husband these days, taking the family everywhere and never so much as looking out of the corner of his eye at any woman other than his wife.

It would seem that our approach to life in those days was merely an earlier version of the present obsession for togetherness with one distinct advantage. Then, ages didn't form the arbitrary dividing line they do today. Mama, of her own free will, waited to start me to school until I was seven because the fall after my sixth birthday I came down with a severe attack of whooping cough, making it seem unwise (to her) for me to undertake the ordeal of learning. Again on her own initiative, she started Sister a year early so I would have company. It was an arrangement to which Sister did not take kindly; not that she minded the early introduction to school—rather it was because she was deemed too young to take turns riding in front and guiding Nell and must always sit behind me, carrying the lunch box. Neither the school directors nor teacher questioned Mama's right to arrange the matter to her own satisfaction.

In those days, we did not have junior church where we attended services separate from our parents. Instead, we sat between them during the sermon, learning early to restrain our tendency to wiggle. I don't recall that we were allowed even the solace of a pencil and piece of paper on which to scribble should we grow restless. And certainly we knew better than to laugh at any older or eccentric person who might do strange or unpredictable things during the service.

As a result, we came to see society for what it was—an integration of many kinds of people, a mingling of all ages and both sexes. Life was a continuing thing, and those who lived it should, like Janus, possess two faces—one looking back on the young, representing the way you have traveled; the other turned forward in the direction of age and the destination ahead.

Naturally, we gave no time to considering this profound philosophy. If we gave the matter any thought at all it was merely to be glad that, just in case Mrs. Vivian saw fit to ask Mama to Sunday dinner, we children would automatically be included.

XV.

Winter Harvest

WINTER was not entirely a time for resting on our laurels and for catching up on our visiting. There was also work to be done. Part of this, of course, was the daily care which must be given the poultry and stock, a matter of routine and scarcely thought about. The real excitement came when we put up ice.

January was the best month for the enterprise; by then the long stretch of cold weather natural to the season had made the ice good and thick. The thicker, the better. I have heard Papa brag about twenty-inch ice, but I believe that was the exception rather than the rule. Papa seemed to know the precise time by instinct.

"I think we'll put up ice tomorrow," he would announce.

Of course, his statement was provisional. It must be a clear day and cold, but not raw or with snow or bitter wind. Nobody expected the workers to handle melting ice, nor did you want them to face snow or a cutting wind. There was nearly always one day exactly right for the venture—a bonus of nature, as it were, sent to enable the prudent to harvest one of her gifts.

For ice was, indeed, a bonus of nature. And, as with her other benefits to mankind, you had to put in some good hard work and ingenuity in order to take advantage of it.

Having made up his mind, Papa would go to the phone and talk with various neighbors who would agree to send their hands (or come themselves, in case they were younger and more active). This, of course, was contingent on whether they "owed" Papa work or whether Papa would, in turn, send our hand to help when and if needed. This pooling of resources was highly convenient; it gave a large working force when needed without making it necessary to keep extra men around when there was nothing much to be done.

Naturally, I would not know, first hand, the actual details of cutting the ice, dragging it ashore, loading it in the wagons. That was man's work, and I don't suppose a woman ever laid eyes upon the process. Thoreau saw fit to mention it in *Walden*, but dismisses the whole matter by saying, "They divided it into cakes by methods too well known to require description."

And who am I to outdo Thoreau. All I can say is, in some way that I do not understand and that I never witnessed, the ice was sawed into blocks, grappled with hooks, and dragged to the shore, where it was then loaded into wagons and brought to the icehouse.

This was a circular hole in the ground perhaps twenty feet deep and as wide across, although I cannot vouch for the exact dimensions. All I remember is that, at the time, it looked like a tremendously big excavation to me. It was lined with bricks, and I believe, the bottom was nothing more than hard-packed earth, thus providing a drainage system for the inevitable melting of the ice. But I refuse to be pinned down to details. I do know there was a pointed roof, made of corrugated tin. Once—and only once—I tried sliding down this incline.

When the workers came to the icehouse with their chunks of ice, they packed them in it after the manner of fashioning a good casserole dish—a layer of clean straw, a layer of ice, fitted in just so, and then a layer of straw until, at last, the icehouse was filled. The final layer was a thick one of straw.

Putting up ice is chilly business, so Mama kept a great kettle of coffee ready on the back of the range. The men would come in at intervals to warm themselves and drink coffee and maybe exchange their wet gloves for a dry pair. When dinnertime came, they all sat down to a first-rate meal, as good as the one Mama prepared for the Presiding Elder or other distinguished guests. This was no more than right; not only were these men doing difficult and uncomfortable work, but they were contributing to our comfort as well.

For ice, beyond any doubt, did add to the pleasures of life. You stored it in the proper season, and then it was there, ready to use when summer came. You did this just as you put away, in season, fruits and vegetables in order that you might have them in winter, when they were not growing. A harvest in reverse, as it were.

When summer came, it was waiting to give you comfort and delight. A thing altogether worth any trouble one might have taken to harvest it, paying dividends far beyond what one could hope for. Again Thoreau marvels that a bucket of water soon becomes putrid, but frozen, it remains sweet forever. Not given to reading Thoreau, we merely accepted the miracle without wondering about it.

When you had your own ice, you used it lavishly. The icebox sat on the back porch. A big wooden box, it had a lid which lifted to reveal the ice compartment. Below were the shelves for storing food—milk, butter, cottage cheese, fruits, tomatoes in season, melons. In short, any food which was the better for being chilled was sure to find its way into the icebox. Mama's standard gift to anyone sick or bereaved was a bowl of fruit gelatin. I can see it, sitting in the icebox to congeal, so that Mama could take it, together with her own comforting words. To this day my first reaction to the news that a friend is ill or in difficulty is to whip up a bowl of gelatin.

You watched the icebox carefully, not wanting it to run out of ice because not only did the food inside suffer if this happened but it took the icebox longer to cool off again.

"Icebox needs filling," Mama would say at breakfast.

So the hand, probably shadowed by Brother, would go to the icehouse and dig around in the straw until he came upon the hoarded hunks. These he would pitch out of the door, load them onto the wheelbarrow, and trundle them to the house. They must be washed at the hydrant (nobody in his right mind would think of putting dirty ice into the box). Once this was done, they were put into the icebox. We were in the cooling business once more.

Papa had rigged up an ingenious device which carried the melted water away through a pipe inserted in the porch floor directly to a tree in the back yard. Never have I seen a tree thrive so well as that one. We thought this very clever of Papa. Everyone else we knew had to empty the pan which sat under the icebox to catch the melted ice. This was an abomination— you were always forgetting it and letting it run over. Or, even if you remembered, the water splashed over you as you carried the pan to the door. More often than not, someone remembered just as you were ready to go to church, and what a mess that turned out to be.

We used ice, when summer came, with a reckless lavishness good for our souls. We liked our iced tea glasses filled to the point where the ice "froze our noses." I am sure if we tried to use home-harvested ice now, we'd all come down with some mysterious plague and probably die like flies. Then either we were made of sterner stuff or those bygone germs lacked the authority inherent in their modern brothers. I know, personally, of only one case where a family sickened from using their own ice, and they got it from The River instead of a proper home pond. And we all said, what could you expect! Goodness only knows what had been dumped there.

And, of course, there was ice cream.

In those days before people worried about calories, nobody considered ice cream fit to eat unless it was made of whole milk and pure cream. It was all to the good if you had to cut the cream out of the crock with a knife. You started from there, adding eggs to the boiled custard made from the whole milk. After that, it was strictly up to you to take off in any direction your taste—or imagination—might dictate.

Freezing ice cream was a ritual in itself. This was usually done on the back porch or, at our house, on a goodish sized slab of concrete in the back yard, a spot considered ideal because you could let the melting ice and salt run out without injuring the grass. The container, with the cream to be frozen, was placed inside the freezer, and then a layer of ice was packed in, a bit of coarse salt sprinkled over it, another layer of ice, and so on until the freezer was full. This done, the crank was clamped firmly down and the fun was on.

Traditionally, turning the crank was a job for small boys, who accepted it willingly enough because it meant the right to lick the dasher once the cream was finished. When it got to exactly the right stage (and only an expert, such as Mama or some other good Missouri cook, could qualify here) the lid was removed. This was always a tense moment. What if you weren't very, very careful to clear off all the salty ice before you opened the container! What if it really wasn't hard enough! What if the dasher had got out of its socket and hadn't really kept paddling away in the cream! There were so many hazards one scarcely dared think of them.

But, in spite of our concern, rarely did anything go wrong. The dasher was pulled out, well covered with ice cream, and above the protests of Brother, who had manned the crank, that Mama was scraping every single bit of it off, Mama managed to subtract the amount she thought right and put it back into the freezer. The dasher, with whatever happened to be left on it, was placed on a plate Brother held out to receive it. Mama replaced the lid, made a plug of paper or cloth, put it into the opening in the lid of the freezer and piled on more ice. Somebody ran to fetch an old blanket kept for the purpose, and the freezer, swathed and protected against melting, was left alone until dinner came, and time for eating.

I recall one occasion when Sister and I begged the hired girl —who must have been light-minded or easily persuaded to give in so quickly—to freeze ice cream while Mama was gone to Ladies Aid or some such thing. When she demurred, saying she didn't know how to make the custard, I assured her airily there was nothing to it. I'd do it myself.

Amazingly enough, my custard came off well enough with

nothing worse than a few lumps, which strained out. From there on out, I lost control, with Sister aiding and abetting me and the hired girl either unable or unwilling to protest. Strawberries being in season, I decided to add some of them. There was a single banana in the kitchen, so Sister and I said, "Why not?" The same for a portion of a can of pineapple in the icebox. Having gone that far, there was really no reason to refrain from adding the last of the raspberry jam in the bowl.

The hired man came in for a drink about that time so we bribed him, with promises of delightful eating, to get us ice from the icehouse. Finally we had all in readiness and started turning the crank, taking turns, feeling full of virtue and accomplishment.

We failed to realize that ice cream, in freezing, expands. It was not long until the freezer was overfull, for which there is only one sure solution. We removed the lid, being careful about brushing all the salty ice away first, spooned out some of the mixture, replaced the lid, and started turning the crank once more. As we did so, we ate the portion we had removed, finding it more than justified our hopes. Never, we were sure, had such delicious ice cream been made in all the history of Missouri cooking.

Before long, we knew we must repeat the process. Off with the lid, out with some excess cream, back with the lid, and turn, turn, turn the crank. This batch, we said, smacking our lips, was even better than the first for it was more nearly frozen.

The third time we did this, for some reason we could not explain, the concoction did not taste quite so good. Wisdom would have dictated that we throw away this sample or, had it been the day of commercial freezers, store it in the freezing compartment. But we had been taught not to waste, to clean up our plates, and besides, it was childhood's inherent right to eat whatever stuck to the dasher. We ate again.

After the first two samplings, the hired girl refused to eat more, a decision we thought most foolish. By the time Mama came home the cream was frozen and covered properly and the hired girl, who knew all along she shouldn't have allowed us to go on that cooking spree, was putting supper on the table, trying not to look the guilt she felt.

It was a meal of which Sister and I did not partake, not even the dessert we had prepared. Very white around the gills, we took massive doses of soda water and went upstairs to bed. In separate rooms. The very sight of each other reminded us of ice cream.

I never thought to ask anyone how he liked our creation.

I remember feeling very sorry for our town cousins who had to buy their ice from a local dealer. It had been made artificially and was shipped in from somewhere. Mama said it "had a taste." Besides, you couldn't chip it off with the reckless abandon we employed when we served ourselves to ice at our house. You couldn't hold it on breathless summer days, wrapped in a piece of clean cloth, tossing it from hand to hand until you were numb with cold. You couldn't make big pitchers of lemonade at will because town mamas were sure to call. "Now shut that ice-box door and don't be wasting ice. It's forty cents a hundred."

The very idea of having to save ice! It was like air—the common right of all. We had it at our back door. I am sure we regarded those underprivileged town kin with some of the cool arrogance the Haves reserve for the Have-nots, or with the disapproval the ants felt for the improvident grasshoppers. For goodness sakes, our attitude implied, why didn't people get busy and store ice when it was there for the taking.

The icehouse had varied uses beyond that for which it was originally intended. It was a wonderful place to play on hot summer days—cool, with the slightly damp straw underfoot, it gave us a hint of the refrigerated air we now take for granted. It was also useful for storing watermelons, especially for big company dinners. The melons were picked the day before. Papa never would have stooped so low as to plug one—that was no sport at all. Like shooting sitting ducks. Besides, once you cut out a portion, be it ever so small, the melon lost flavor. He *thumped* them with his forefinger, the resulting sound telling him all he needed to know. "This is good," he would say of one and, "This is green," of another. Or, even, "This is too ripe."

For the life of me I could never detect the slightest difference, but rarely did he make a mistake.

The ones pronounced right for the purpose were buried in the straw in the icehouse, down close to the ice. Then in midafternoon they were brought out—with everyone protesting he couldn't swallow a bite—taken to the concrete slab in the back yard, placed on a table, and cut open. At the right stage of ripeness, they made a nice hollow thud when opened. The cut seemed to run ahead of the knife, as if the melon knew it was fulfilling its destiny, its reason for being. It simply couldn't wait to be eaten, to hear people say, "I do believe this is the best melon I ever tasted."

Once the melons were cut everyone who couldn't possibly eat another bite fell to, using salt or not, according to his own persuasion in the matter. Of course, the children spilled the juice down the front of their clothes and mothers washed their faces, and their little fronts, and said, "There, I knew I shouldn't let you wear your best clothes today." Finally the last bite was gone and the rinds were gathered up in a tub and carried off to the hogs, a most natural and appreciative garbage disposal. Somebody made haste to wash down the concrete and we all staggered back to our places, saying weren't those melons good—that came of eating them in season, and cold enough to hurt your teeth.

By and by, we bought an electric refrigerator. People came calling just to see it, a fact which they freely admitted.

"We hear you have a new electric icebox," they would say. "My, my—"

Good etiquette demanded the visitor ask to see it, just as one asked to see a new baby in the house. Once a feud, lasting for years, started because a woman bought a new electric icebox and her next door neighbor (and supposedly, closest friend) never mentioned it.

"Never even mentioned it!" the outraged owner reported.

"Imagine that! Right next door to you, and she never even mentioned it!"

It was hard to believe a person could be so rude and thoughtless.

There were many subtle ways of cutting the owner down to size while all the time pretending to admire the new acquisition. For instance, instead of saying wasn't it wonderful, and such a good thing not to have to put up ice in winter and wait for the hand to fill the box in summer, and so convenient not to have to empty that pan—instead of saying all these things common courtesy demanded, now and then some misanthrope would merely take a long look and ask, "Does it work?"

Occasionally, once a woman had hers in place, the dark rumor would go around that she had bought it from a junk dealer in Kansas City and it couldn't be depended upon to keep things even mildly cool. Real friends hung back, unwilling to verify these unpleasant allegations, but those not so dedicated in their friendship (and, of course, the envious and the scoffers) made special trips to verify the facts for themselves. The trick was to ask for a drink of water and then follow the hostess as she went to comply with the request. If she opened the icebox door and got out a tray of ice (all frozen in little squares, and wasn't that funny!) and, by sheer strength and awkwardness, extracted some from the tray, they had to believe the newfangled thing might just be all right. *Might*, understand. It was working now, but by tomorrow no one could be sure. If, however, she brought a pitcher of water from the icebox, there was sure to be some question as to whether the contraption really made ice or she used the supply from the icehouse for real cooling and kept this new acquisition more for storage.

Served her right, the mean ones said, if the latter suspicion proved true. She should have stuck to her old icebox. At least, you could depend on that. Anyway, things just sort of tasted better when you cooled them with real ice.

And sometimes I think they might have had a point.

"I don't care what you say," Sister burst out not long ago. "That ice was colder."

I was all set to laugh at her, to say ice was ice. But then came back to me—tea in the tall glass with the ice pressed against my nose; ice cream, slowly congealing in the freezer on the concrete in the back yard; the watermelons, firm and sweet and cold between your aching teeth—I thought of these, and I wondered.

Perhaps she was right, after all.

XVI.

But Once a Year

I DON'T believe it used to start so early.

The Christmas season, I mean. It came in officially, at least in the minds of us children, when Mr. Brunkhorst set up the clock in his store window. On the top was a Santa Claus head which went wagging back and forth, marking off the seconds. No notices reminded us of the number of shopping days left until Christmas. Gift buying was a matter which we took care of at a rather leisurely pace. I remember one year we waited until Christmas Eve Day, and then barely made it home before the Big Snow came. Papa put the car in the garage where it stayed for almost a week. This stands out as one of the nicest Christmases we ever had, shut in as we were, without even the mail carrier coming until two days after Christmas.

Logs burned brightly in the fireplace. We played the victrola until Mama said she was ready to lose her mind; we telephoned friends and relatives several times a day; we listened, without apology, to every ring that came in over the line. And of course, Mama cooked all our favorite dishes.

It was also a good time to read our new Christmas books and reread the old favorites. Our house had a spot ideal for winter reading—a couch in the upstairs hall under a window overlooking the front yard. A bookcase stood nearby. Here, fortified by a plate of apples and a bowl of popcorn, we could sprawl for hours, utterly comfortable, completely content, lost to time and space, our eyes glued to the printed page.

Not one of us considered this an unexciting way to spend Christmas.

In fact, Christmas, like life in general, was simpler then. Not better, not worse. Just simpler. And a great deal easier on the pocketbook, to say nothing of the blood pressure.

Even though we might delay a bit on the shopping, the other preparations had started well ahead of time. The fruit cakes were made early in December and put away to ripen. Mama used a cherished recipe which called for dried apples. These we had grown on our own trees, and then, in the heat of August, we peeled them, cut them into small sections, and put them on a slab in the sun to dry. They had to be covered with mosquito netting to keep away the flies and other insects; they had to be turned every day; they had to be kept in the direct rays of the sun; they had to be brought in every evening before the dew fell. They were, in short, treated with much the same tender loving care accorded a newborn babe.

But, like a well-brought-up child, they paid dividends. When we were ready to make the fruit cake, we soaked them over night and then the next morning candied them, using plenty of sugar, cooking them over a slow fire. When they were finished they were chewy, moist, a bright amber in color, and utterly delectable. It was a wonder they could bring themselves to blend with the ordinary raisins and spices and other ingredients of the Christmas cake. I still make the cake, using commercially dried apples, but the flavor is not the same. The difference is subtle, like comparing a recording of a symphony concert with the real thing.

There was, also, mincemeat. For this you butchered a beef, one you had raised from a calf, which had never had a cross word spoken to it in all its life. This slaughter started a ritual known as "trading quarters." Some neighbor who had butchered at another time and had let you have a "quarter" was now repaid in kind. If you had received a front "quarter" from him, of course that's what he got in return. The hind "quarter," considered the choice one, was always kept at home at Christmas time. A portion of this we used in making mincemeat.

I remember neither the recipe nor the process except in the vaguest sort of way. The meat was cooked first—this I know. Afterward raisins and currants and spices were added. Also some apple cider which was first boiled down. I think Mama, possessed with the spirit of adventure, might occasionally have tossed in pickled peach juice and maybe some canned cherries and—yes— I think a few fine slithers of apples when baking time came. When she had the mixture to her liking, she packed it into stone jars or crocks and stored them in the cellar, there to wait their ultimate destiny, the Christmas pies.

But of all the preparations, the animal cookies are the most fondly remembered.

Mama made them from a recipe given her by Papa's mother, using the cookie cutters which had also been hers. A sugar cookie dough it was, rolled to paper thinness and cut into the shapes of dogs and horses and camels and rabbits and chickens and reindeer. There were also stars and Christmas trees, but we liked the animal ones best, going back as they did to the legend of that first Christmas when the animals were said to have knelt in worship before the baby Jesus.

Once the cookies were out of the oven, the work had barely started. They must then be iced with white frosting and decorated. I have spent hours setting raisin eyes in the heads of those cookies, and still more time swirling colored icing in loops on trees and stars. Then, red and green sugar must be sprinkled over the entire surface. When they were finally finished, the cookies were almost (but not quite) too beautiful to eat.

Of course, it was necessary to double or sometimes triple the recipe for both cookies and icing on important occasions like Christmas. At such times Mama, finding herself lost in the intricacies of three times one and three-fourths cups, turned to Papa for help. He was a genius in math, but occasionally he would give the wrong answer, just to tease—a deception Mama always caught because it was accompanied by a grin, mischievous yet tender, not devoid of complacency. As if he were saying to himself, "Ah, this dear little woman I married. What would she do without me!"

A very smart woman, my mother.

A cousin once said, "If I woke up in Hong Kong on the Fourth of July and saw one of Aunt Mollie's Christmas cookies, I'd figure the calendar was all wrong and start my Christmas shopping on the spot."

Since we always ate Christmas dinner at Grandma's house, the food we prepared was more of a supplementary nature than the main ingredients for the feast. In this category we classed ham. A sugar-cured ham, considered a great delicacy now, was accepted as commonplace by all Missouri cooks, Mama included. Our smokehouse held any number of them, cured by Papa's own recipe, swathed in layers of paper and cloth, and then hung cheek by jowl with the less glamorous sides of bacon.

Ham, for us, was a staple item of diet, as rice is for the Chinese. No sooner was one finished than Papa cut another, this procedure being considered too difficult for a woman. Fried ham was standard for breakfast; it was always accompanied by "red gravy," a delectable liquid made from the residue of fat and drippings left in the skillet after the ham was fried, diluted with a suitable amount of water, heated to the boiling point and poured over the meat in the platter. Mouth-watering, this ambrosia came to its full peak of perfection when ladled over hot biscuits.

Boiled ham was another thing. After a careful scrubbing it was boiled on top of the stove and then finished off by baking in the oven with a coating of brown sugar and probably sweet peach pickle juice and dotted with cloves. Mama always kept a baked ham on hand "just in case," using the same forethought I employ in stocking up cans of tuna and pork and beans.

When I think of the price we pay now for sugar-cured hams which are, at best, only poor imitations of the ones Papa used to store in our smokehouse, I marvel at the way in which we took them as no more than our due. Sometimes I wonder if the measure of a good life could be the number of lovely things we can take for granted.

At school, preparations were also in full swing as we made gifts for our parents and each other (wobbly works of art achieved with crayons and paper or bits of cloth smuggled from home). By the time we were able to present them, we were almost exhausted from the burden of trying to keep them secret from the intended recipient.

We had a program at school, small and without pretensions. I do not remember that we ever had a Christmas tree there or that the teacher gave us gifts or a treat. I think we usually took up a collection, fancying we were keeping the whole thing a great secret, and bought some sort of a present for him. I am sure it was a dreadfully unsuitable necktie, or something else equally inappropriate. Why our parents did not take a hand in the matter I am not prepared to say.

There was a program at our church on Christmas Eve. Of course we all had a part in it. I remember once Brother almost wrecked it. He was to hang up his stocking. Just that, nothing more. Sister and some of her friends were slated to sing a song about him.

Funny thing, nobody thought about a dress rehearsal, even though Brother was to wear his pajamas, which, for no reason any of us ever knew, he called his "jiggers." I guess we just trusted to luck and a child's natural instinct for acting, if we gave the matter any thought at all.

Usually our programs were simple in nature, but this time we had gone big time and had a curtain, made from white sheets someone had brought from home and pinned across a wire. A few older members thought this innovation rather shocking, but we didn't even listen to them. Progress was not to be stopped by a few old fogies. Everyone settled down in his place, expecting a real production.

The pianist struck the keys, the signal for the number in which Brother was to appear. Mama leaned forward in her seat, trying not to look smug at having *two* children in one performance. Just then the curtain parted and Brother's head appeared while he held the folds of the curtain tight across his middle.

"Mama," he yelled, "they're trying to make me put on my jiggers and it's not time to go to bed."

Everyone howled. Mama's ears turned pink. Brother disappeared with a speed that could mean only one thing—he had been yanked forcibly from the rear. We heard a round of brief, whispered argument behind the curtain. An agonized stillness, which the audience sat out with as much calmness as it could muster. And then, the curtain opened—a little jerkily, but still it opened—and there was Brother, subdued and amenable, standing by a wobbly make-believe mantel, holding his stocking. Yes, and wearing his pajamas. Someone—maybe the Sunday school teacher, an authority ranking close to the preacher and the superintendent—had evidently persuaded him it was a privilege to wear "jiggers" in a Christmas program. Or maybe they had merely assured him it did not mean he would have to go to bed and miss all the fun; or, what is even more likely, Sister had bribed him by promising him her "treat" when the time came for passing them out.

The song did not fare as well. The singers, so filled with giggles they could barely get the words out, galloped through the number at such a great pace the pianist had difficulty keeping up with them. Brother easily remained the star of the show.

Christmas dinner was, by custom unbroken, eaten with Mama's parents. Aunts and uncles and cousins trooped in, and it was just like a family reunion with everyone talking at once and food all over the place. There was one difference here, however, for while an ordinary reunion was an end in itself, Christmas Day, for us, was a sort of interlude, set in suspension between what we had and what was yet to be. As a reminder of the first part of Christmas we wore a gift—a new hair ribbon or maybe a locket or bracelet; and to our hearts we hugged the knowledge that tonight there was still the Three Groves Christmas tree.

Papa had belonged to this little rural church before he went over to the Methodists with Mama. Like the school we attended, Papa's father had helped to found it. The smart cousin went there. Certainly we came not as outsiders, nor were we without debt to it. Here was held each Christmas night the annual program. Without this, Christmas would have ended with the dinner at Grandma's and the inevitable letdown which comes of knowing the great adventure is finished.

As it was, we went about all Christmas Day not only enjoying the present but having the added zest which anticipation gives. Once we were home from Grandma's, we dressed in our best, a privilege denied us during the day, and set off once more. We were going to call on our other grandparents, Papa's mother and father, to wish them merry Christmas. This was not the uninhibited experience a visit to Mama's parents offered. Here we were quiet and dignified and certainly less impulsive; here we did not interrupt anybody, not even the smart cousin in whose home our grandparents lived. We visited, we exchanged gifts. The interlude was good for us; in effect it said, "Be quiet, spirit, so that you may be able to endure the joy which is to come."

Recently a cousin said, "I used to feel sorry for all those poor deprived people who didn't have the Three Groves Christmas tree to go to on Christmas night."

For, of course, we brought home assorted cousins with us, to spend a few days of vacation and to attend the program.

"Do you remember that time we went in a sled?" he continued.

If there was snow, we did occasionally go in a sled with a couple of brisk horses pulling it. Papa drove and the rest of us sat on blankets thrown over the straw in the bottom of the sled. I think we sang all the way there and back. All except me, for I was supposed to be quiet so that I would be in good voice when the time came for me to say my piece. At this time I felt the price of stardom came too high.

The tree there was the biggest in the world. Of that we were all convinced. Also, it had real candles on it, a custom continued long after other institutions had deemed them too dangerous for use in community gatherings. Here, the members of the congregation solved the problem very nicely by setting one man

—it was always the same one—to watching those candles. Equipped with a bucket of water and a long pole to which a piece of cloth was attached, he sat—immobile, alert, watchful. If a candle so much as gave the slightest indication that it might have burned down low enough to catch the tree on fire, he rose with unhurried and purposeful dignity and touched it with his improvised fire extinguisher. Fire in that small crowded wooden building would have been a disaster too tragic to contemplate. We never gave the matter a thought. Year after year this man sat there guarding us, while we accepted his watchfulness as we accepted sunlight and air and all the rest of heaven's gifts.

Sister says there was a trick to watching those candles. If you peered at them through half-closed eyes, they looked bigger, more numerous, and, also, seemed to twinkle like far-off stars. I think I remember best the smell of it, the pungent aromatic odor of candles so close to cedar; or, perhaps, the voice of the superintendent intoning the numbers on the program until he came, at last, to me. I was never at ease until I was finished—there were so many things I must remember: To push my braids over my shoulder, so that they hung down my back; to walk up to my place, and back, with unhurried ease; to speak clearly and loudly. Not only was I, in a manner of speaking, on unfamiliar ground here, but this program was also inherently more serious than the one in our own church. I can't imagine Brother protesting about wearing his "jiggers" here, if, indeed, such a light-minded number would be allowed in the first place.

But I think the part we all remembered best, looked forward to the most keenly, was the giving of treats.

These came in brown paper sacks of truly heroic proportions. Never have I seen such size or variety of contents. All the while the program was going on you could see them under the tree. When the last speech had been said, the last note of the final song had died down (I have yet to hear any group sing "Joy to the World" with the spirit the congregation at Three Groves put into it), the real business—for us—of the evening began. The superintendent called forward several helpers and then, from a list in his hand, read off the names of the children. As your name was called, you walked up, took your great sack (folded over neatly at the top), said "thank you," and walked back to your place.

The first child ventured only the stealthiest peep; after a few more received theirs, we grew bolder. Presently there was a noise all over the building, like a wind in the forest, growing louder by the moment, as children began to dig into their sacks. You'd think we hadn't eaten a bite in weeks.

In my earlier, more innocent years, I don't believe I ever gave any thought as to how the sacks got under the tree. Maybe I thought they grew there, from seed left the preceding Christmas. Like the program itself, they were a sort of unearned increment, a bonus coming after you had every reason to believe Christmas was over for another year. Even then I suspected dimly that it all went too fast.

Finally I found out the real story back of those sacks. It was worse than learning the true identity of Santa Claus, because I had always had some mental reservations about that old boy, dating back to the time when I opened Mama's closet door and a doll fell out on my head. It was the same one I had seen in Mr. Brunkhorst's store, and begged for, and Mama said maybe Santa would bring it to me. What was it doing in Mama's closet now if Santa was supposed to be looking after the matter?

So I wasn't exactly unprepared for the truth about Santa. But it did sort of hit me below the belt when I found out about the treat.

Our papas paid for them. That's why we got our sacks—every last one of us. The year of discovery was one of disillusionment for me.

"What's the matter?" a kind lady asked, seeing my sack still unopened when all the other children were going through theirs like beavers collecting logs for a dam. "Don't you like what we've put in it?"

"Oh, yes, ma'am," I assured her, with more haste and emphasis than the answer required. How was she to know she had given me a double blow? Not only did the fathers pay for the treats, but human hands arranged them. I handed mine over to a visiting cousin who was, even at that moment, regarding it as a refugee child might look at the first food he has seen in days. I was praised for my generosity, words which did nothing to raise my spirits, knowing they were ill-deserved.

But by and by I grew up, and went no more to the Three Groves program except, of course, in memory. There I still see the brightness of the candles, hear the rustling of the sacks, feel the excitement. And being granted the insight which is the gift of the backward look, I forgive the good people of the church for ruling that the treat must be paid for. I can even appreciate the magnitude of their accomplishment. In their own way, with no apparent effort, they succeeded in implementing the great wish of the world.

They made Christmas last a little longer.

Sister confesses she used to play a game, watching the candles on the tree, giving each a name. Some twinkled brightly, some flickered, some burned out quickly. Others, let us face it, were a bit on the drippy side. Naturally the best and most steadfast always bore the names of kin. These relatives, she felt, were also watching her, winking their approval, assuring her that though absent in body, they were, in spirit, enjoying the occasion with her.

It is a fancy I like to recall now.

Once we were a clan whose center was in the little town. Now we are scattered, yet there still remains a clan on the hill over-looking the town. Here they lie in unaccustomed quiet and inactivity, those quick, impulsive, eager people, each one's place marked by a slab bearing his name and the stark statistics of birth and death.

Perhaps, though, like Sister's candles, the spirit, the essence of them comes out at times, there to commune with each other, remembering happy times, recalling past joys.

It could just be. We were never a family to remain quiet for long.